MAKING SENSE OF ULTRA-REALISM

Ultra-Realism is one of the most exciting and innovative theoretical frameworks to have emerged from criminology in a long time. But its roots in continental philosophy and theoretical psychoanalysis are relatively unfamiliar to the discipline and quite different from its usual intellectual wellsprings. Consequently, ultra-realism has acquired a somewhat unfair reputation for being dense, inaccessible and intimidating to newcomers. Making Sense of Ultra-Realism *corrects this in one fell swoop. A mash-up of high theory and popular culture, Kotzé and Lloyd offer the uninitiated a highly accessible guide to ultra-realism, making foreign concepts and terminology familiar by quilting them through movies and television shows such as the* Avengers *films,* Fight Club *and* Game of Thrones *among others. Fun, thought-provoking and intellectually accomplished, it will be useful for established academics and undergraduate students alike. Quite simply, it is the book that ultra-realism needs.*

–Dr Thomas Raymen, Associate Professor of Criminology, Northumbria University, UK

This book is a straightforward and accessible introduction to ultra-realism. This body of theory represents by far the most significant shift in criminological sense-making in recent years. It propels criminology into the twenty-first century, bringing with it a set of new, innovative conceptual frameworks and analytical tools. This text helps students of criminology – both within and outside of formal education – get to grips with ultra-realism. It uses relatable, contemporary examples that will resonate with them, and as such, facilitate their understanding. Theory can often be intimidating, abstract and impenetrable, but this book breaks through all of those barriers. Engaging and approachable texts like this help students see the real-world applications of theory. It shows them how they can use ultra-realism in their studies and beyond to make sense of the late modern world we find ourselves in, and begin to tackle the harms that emerge within it.

–Professor Elizabeth Yardley, Professor of Criminology, Birmingham City University, UK

An enjoyable book that will be very useful for academics and students interested in exploring ultra-realism. The use of examples from popular culture work effectively to engage the audience and explain complex ideas. Ultra-realism is a theoretical framework with significant scope for development across criminology and the social sciences, and this book provides the opportunity for readers to appreciate its capacity and, I hope, take it in to realms of thinking where it has not previously been used.

–Professor Zoë James, Professor of Criminology,
University of Plymouth, UK

MAKING SENSE OF ULTRA-REALISM

Contemporary Criminological Theory Through the Lens of Popular Culture

BY

JUSTIN KOTZÉ
Teesside University, UK

And

ANTHONY LLOYD
Teesside University, UK

emerald
PUBLISHING

United Kingdom – North America – Japan – India
Malaysia – China

Emerald Publishing Limited
Howard House, Wagon Lane, Bingley BD16 1WA, UK

First edition 2022

British Library Cataloguing in Publication Data
A catalogue record for this book is available from the British Library

ISBN: 978-1-80117-170-0 (Print)
ISBN: 978-1-80117-169-4 (Online)
ISBN: 978-1-80117-171-7 (Epub)

CONTENTS

LIST OF FIGURES

ABOUT THE CONTRIBUTORS

Dr Justin Kotzé is Senior Lecturer in Criminology and Criminal Justice at Teesside University, UK. Justin's research interests are wide-ranging, and he has published work on social harm, violence, the consumption of steroids and the commodification of abstinence. He is also the author of *The Myth of the 'Crime Decline': Exploring Change and Continuity in Crime and Harm* (Routledge, 2019), co-editor of *Zemiology: Reconnecting Crime and Social Harm* (Palgrave, 2018) and co-author of *Lockdown: Social Harm in the Covid-19 Era* (Palgrave, 2021).

Dr Anthony Lloyd is Associate Professor in Criminology and Sociology at Teesside University, UK. His research interests primarily focus on work and labour markets. His research also includes investigation of urban sociology and migration. He is particularly interested in blending analysis of the workplace with emerging theoretical frameworks around critical criminology and social harm to understand experiences of low-paid, insecure and flexible forms of labour. He has published widely in this area and is the author of *The Harms of Work: An Ultra-Realist Account of the Service Economy* (Bristol University Press, 2018) and co-author of *Lockdown: Social Harm in the Covid-19 Era* (Palgrave, 2021).

FOREWORD

Ultra-realism was really born of frustration. For us, much of criminology is polluted by out-of-date ideas and the sort of dour abstracted empiricism that fills databases with little more than quantified confirmation bias. What should be a field of dynamism, creativity and revealing intellectual discovery is beset by a range of tranquilising conventions that actively prevent the discipline moving forward to better represent the complex realities that today surround the abstract concepts of crime, harm and victimisation. Strapped firmly to the unchallengeable domain assumptions forced by various cultural activists to the forefront of the discipline, ultra-realists decided that the criminological agenda looks badly misaligned with popular social and political concerns.

Our project began quite simply as an attempt to represent more accurately the world in which people experience crime and harm and in which politicians and social administrators react. The early ultra-realists felt weighed down by the discipline's tendency to focus almost exclusively on social reaction rather than the contexts that underpinned crime and harm. These contexts needed to be revisited because political, economic, cultural and social life had changed quite substantially since the times in which the discipline's most influential texts had been written. Early ultra-realists knew that the suggestion to revisit what had become sacred ground might upset vested interests within the discipline, but they were unprepared for the hostility of the reaction that ensued. We were resilient enough to field the criticism, but we were very worried about leading students into the sort of censorious reaction that could damage their careers. But, of course, that decision is not ours to make, and the authors of this book number amongst a growing body of researchers who without fear decided to be faithful to their own curiosity. The discipline still refuses to celebrate them in the way it did its rather mediocre figures of the past, but that, thankfully, is not their main concern.

While the ultra-realist literature can often appear quite abstract, in the vast majority of cases the work of ultra-realist researchers is rooted in face-to-face investigative work with criminals, 'deviants' and victims. Actually meeting and getting to know active criminals tends to display just how idealistic and unworldly so much criminological theory really is. Despite what critical criminologists have often claimed, many criminals believe their crimes have absolutely no political resonance. When violent offenders, drug dealers, thieves and fraudsters commit crimes, they are really not trying to fight back against the unfairness of capitalism. The true realities that make up the probabilistic contexts in which crime and harm are played out are far more complex.

We had no particularly grand ambitions when we set out on our project. We simply wanted to carry out our research on real-world crime problems, publish it in books and journals, and generally add to the canon of criminological scholarship. On occasion we were mildly acerbic when discussing the empirical and theoretical work of some of our disciplinary colleagues, but at no stage did we over-step the mark or go beyond disciplinary conventions. However, as time passed it became clear that some notable figures within the discipline were keen to censor and misrepresent our work. We were simply not interested in reproducing the discipline's dominant orthodoxies. We wanted to revisit reality and at the same time use new ideas from intellectual fields usually ignored by criminologists. We even had the temerity to introduce a handful of new analytical concepts. We developed a reputation as outsiders.

In truth, this probably has something to do with our shared class background, which clashed with academic criminology's tendency to reflect the concerns – and indeed the underlying fears – of middle-class left-liberals who dominate the discipline. Our outsider status created a range of problems for us, but we also managed to make contacts with others who were equally keen to poke their heads outside the main door of liberalism's criminological cathedral in order to accurately represent the real world.

Perhaps the most gratifying part of our long careers has been to work closely with many talented, open-minded and intellectually ambitious colleagues who, like us, have been willing to defy convention and follow the intellectual track wherever it takes them. Two of those colleagues are the authors of this book, and many others are mentioned within it. Some of these colleagues were once our students, and it has given us a huge amount of pleasure to watch them develop into world-leading criminologists. We still read their work carefully, and the sheer intellectual breadth and depth of their various studies and analyses gives us a vague sense that, even though criminology continues to display manifold problems, there are sections of the discipline that continue to forge ahead to illuminate contemporary crime problems.

For us, Kotzé's and Lloyd's *Making Sense of Ultra-Realism* will act as the definitive introduction to ultra-realism for some time to come. Kotzé and Lloyd have both contributed enormously to the development of ultra-realism, and they know the field inside out. The book itself, as you're about to discover, is both accessible and a pleasure to read. The authors utilise a range of movies and TV series to show how a number of ultra-realism's core ideas can shed light on various features of everyday life.

In our long academic careers numerous open-minded students from all sorts of backgrounds have told us quite clearly that when it comes to understanding crime and harm, ultra-realism makes far more sense than other schools of criminological thought. There's no doubt that this book is an invaluable introductory text for students at all levels, but the fact of the matter is that ultra-realism is for everybody. We have no desire to maintain control over its development. We welcome the involvement of anyone who cares about accurately representing forms of crime and harm in their relevant contexts.

As Kotzé and Lloyd show, there's no need to be intimated by the various abstractions of ultra-realism. With a little work and some imagination, anyone can grasp its core concepts and put them to work explaining various features of the world we live in. We welcome you to the book, and we thank the authors for taking the time to write such an accessible and engaging introduction to the ultra-realist perspective.

Simon Winlow, Professor of Criminology,
Northumbria University, UK
Steve Hall, Emeritus Professor of Criminology
February 2022

ACKNOWLEDGEMENTS

We would like to thank Katy Mathers and her colleagues at Emerald for helping us bring this book to life. For stimulating our interest in ultra-realism, we are eternally indebted to Steve Hall and Simon Winlow; your excellent scholarship, collegiality and unwavering support over the years has been invaluable to us and we are forever grateful. We would also like to acknowledge a debt of gratitude to Philip Whitehead, Georgios A. Antonopoulos, Thomas Raymen, Oliver Smith, Anthony Ellis, Luke Telford, Alexandra Hall, Louise Wattis, Georgios Papanicolaou, Victoria Bell, Daniel Briggs and Mark Bushell for their friendship and continued encouragement. For contributing their valuable insights and helpful study tips, we would like to thank all those students who took the time to share their thoughts and experiences with us. Your participation has certainly helped us in our endeavour to make ultra-realism more accessible and we are sure the reader will benefit immeasurably from your efforts.

Justin Kotzé thanks his co-author Anthony Lloyd for his friendship, support, encouragement and, of course, contribution to this book. It has been a joy to work with you on this publication. Finally, and most importantly, Justin would like to thank his wife, Claire. Thank you for everything you do and for your unfaltering love, support and encouragement.

Anthony Lloyd thanks his co-author Justin Kotzé for the friendship, support and continued collaboration. Most importantly, Anthony would like to thank Jo for, well, everything.

1

INTRODUCTION

INTRODUCTION

This book offers an introduction to the emerging theoretical framework of ultra-realism. The ultra-realist project is a relatively new development within criminological theory and still remains in the margins of the discipline (Hall & Winlow, 2015). Its founders, Steve Hall and Simon Winlow, in attempting to make sense of contemporary problems *as they exist in the world today*, found existing theories and explanations inadequate. Although aspects of criminological theory had proven useful and offered some insights, most interpretations either failed to address motivation and causation or did not appear to correspond with the reality emerging from research. This led to an intellectual search for tools that did provide coherent and logical explanations for the issues they had observed throughout their research (Hall, 1997; Hall, Winlow, & Ancrum, 2008; Winlow, 2001; Winlow & Hall, 2006). Ultimately, their efforts to answer a crucial question – why do some people willingly inflict harm on others in order to further their own expressive or instrumental ends? – moved them away from applying existing theories towards the development of new theoretical and explanatory tools. The aim of the book is to help the reader unpack the various concepts and theoretical tools that make up the body of ultra-realist theory.

Following Hall and Winlow's work, christened 'ultra-realism' around 2015, a small but growing group of criminologists and social scientists who agreed with its aim of offering a realistic interpretation of the problems of crime and harm and were committed to a 'warts and all' presentation of reality as it is began to use and interrogate this theoretical framework (Briggs & Gamero, 2017; Ellis, 2016; Kotzé, 2019; Lloyd, 2018a; Raymen & Smith, 2019; Tudor, 2018). Although marginal within the discipline, ultra-realism is growing and has moved from looking at violence and masculinity to a wide range of issues including workplace harm (Lloyd, 2020), consumer culture (Smith, 2014), lifestyle gambling (Raymen & Smith, 2020), serial murder (Lynes, Kelly, & Uppal, 2019), environmental crisis (Raymen & Smith, 2021), counterfeit fashion (Large, 2018), steroids and performance-enhancing drugs (Hall, 2019; Kotzé & Antonopoulos, 2021), fraud (Tudor, 2019), drug addiction (Briggs & Gamero, 2017), debt (Horsley, 2015), hate crime (James, 2020), politics (Telford, 2022; Winlow et al., 2017) and the COVID-19 pandemic (Briggs, Telford, Lloyd, Ellis, & Kotzé, 2021). It seems that ultra-realism offers a degree of theoretical flexibility that allows its application to a range of contemporary issues. As such, it is also beginning to appear on undergraduate and postgraduate courses.

We have both taught criminological theory to undergraduate and postgraduate students for a number of years now and have incorporated ultra-realism into our modules. Given the breadth of its interdisciplinarity, ultra-realism's component parts often require readers at all levels to engage with subjects and disciplines outside of their area of interest or experience. Ultra-realism draws upon insights from theoretical psychoanalysis, philosophy and moral philosophy, neuroscience, history and criminological theory. This presents a challenge in teaching concepts like transcendental materialism, the pseudo-pacification process, special liberty and others. We have frequently discussed how best to break down these component parts, with examples that work best to hang these new and at times complex ideas in ways that facilitate student understanding. Using examples from popular culture has often helped. This book began as a discussion about how difficult it is to watch films without seeing elements of theory being played out on screen and, in particular, how the *Avengers* offered useful examples of transcendental materialism. From there, we quickly identified other cultural texts that provided useful insight, and we were off and running.

Cultural criminology long ago identified cultural texts as objects of criminological significance (Ferrell, Hayward, & Young, 2015). Academic research acts as a platform for understanding crime and criminology, but a growing recognition exists that other sources of knowledge can also generate pertinent insights (Rafter, 2007). Television and film have recently become central to the emergence of 'pop-criminology' (Rafter, 2007), where criminological theories are explored and representations of crime, criminals and the criminal justice system are dissected (Carrabine, 2008; Rothe & Collins, 2013). Pop criminology also offers insights into audiences (Wattis, 2021). As criminologists, we regularly field questions about serial killers and the latest Netflix documentary which indicates the popularity and reach of streaming services and the public fascination with representations of crime, violence and harm. It also perhaps indicates that most people are unaware of the breadth of criminology as a discipline. Pop-criminology, however, allows for the exploration of criminological theory in relation to media embedded within the ideological framework of contemporary society (Raymen, 2018). Films and television perform ideological work by telling the viewer about crime, society and culture. How we perceive 'good' and 'evil', for example, is connected to the way these concepts are presented within mainstream culture. In this book, we explore some of this ideological work and focus on aspects of popular culture, through TV and film, to explore contemporary developments in criminological theory.

When teaching criminological theory, we have both found it useful to relate concepts to students in various ways, including using characters, scenes and plot from different shows or films. Although we have both learnt a great deal about what students do and do not watch (an entire first year social theory cohort springs to mind who had not seen *The Matrix,* therefore making a postmodernism lecture framed around the film much more challenging), using popular culture can help in terms of understanding theory and concepts and in testing and critiquing theoretical frameworks. For that reason, we have decided to introduce ultra-realist concepts in relation to a range of film and TV series. Our hope is that the reader can follow our analysis and begin to consider other examples that work as representations of each concept, or challenge the utility or accuracy of a concept.

OUTLINE OF THE BOOK

The book begins with a brief introduction to ultra-realism and situates its emergence within the wider context of criminological theory. We outline the perceived limitations of a discipline that has moved away from questions of aetiology and motivation. Having highlighted the influences on ultra-realism, we briefly outline the core concepts of transcendental materialism, the pseudo-pacification process and special liberty. These represent attempts to move beyond existing ideas and concepts and offer tools that potentially explain challenging and troubling issues in the fields of crime and harm. From there, the following chapters each focus on a particular aspect of ultra-realism in relation to a specific film or TV series. In Chapter 3, we set out the transcendental materialist subject as a departure from existing interpretations of subjectivity and do so with reference to Loki, Ultron and Thanos in the *Avengers* films. Using insights from theoretical psychoanalysis and neuroscience, the transcendental materialist position offers a unique interpretation of the complex relationship between the individual, ideology and society. Chapter 4 then focuses on Steve Hall's twin concepts of pseudo-pacification and special liberty. To examine these concepts, the *Pirates of the Caribbean* and *Indiana Jones* films offer useful insights. Pseudo-pacification draws on psychoanalysis and historical analysis to question whether human history is one of increased pacification and civility. It offers a critical interpretation of ways in which drive and libidinal energy are re-directed by social and economic forces but require balance and stabilising effects to prevent eruptions of violence, predatory behaviour and too much self-interested entitlement.

Chapter 5 introduces the concept of fetishistic disavowal through examination of *Game of Thrones*. This chapter considers Slavoj Žižek's concept, a key part of ultra-realist theory, and the 'reversal of ideology'; it asks a fundamental question about how ideology works on the subject in a postmodern culture of cynical distance. Using *Game of Thrones,* we demonstrate the human capacity to repress uncomfortable knowledge in ways that allow us to continue living our lives free from concern about wider harms and inequalities that may be present in the choices we make. In Chapter 6, Dan Brown's novel *Inferno* and its subsequent film adaptation provide insight into the idea of 'enlightened catastrophism' (Dupuy, 2014). This concept asks us to project ourselves into the future to recognise the reality of particular challenges and identify the scale of intervention required to prevent catastrophe. Drawing upon this key concept, ultra-realism's policy relevance is visible in its critical question: what is the level of intervention needed to change something?

In Chapter 7, we examine consumer culture, desire and lack in the context of Chuck Palanhiuk's *Fight Club*. Ultra-realism borrows from theoretical psychoanalysis and the work of Jacques Lacan to understand how we are driven by absence and lack but that desire is directed, through ideology, into outlets such as consumer culture. Here we consider the critical role of the unconscious and the power of ideology through discussion of the self-destructive behaviour presented in the book and film. Our last case study, in Chapter 8, investigates trauma and violent subjectivity through the TV series *Ray Donovan*. Ultra-realist criminology initially emerged from research on violence and masculinity and theoretical development has continued to look at 'violent subjectivity'. Most forms of committed and extreme violence are perpetrated by a small number of men and so insights into the unconscious, trauma, shame and humiliation, as well as the interrelationship between childhood trauma, biography and environment, offer a new way of looking at violence. In Chapter 9, we move from film and TV into the world of criminological research. This chapter demonstrates how the concepts and theories outlined throughout the book have been applied in recent criminological research to show the wide range of contexts and the adaptability of these ideas. We finish with a short conclusion to summarise ultra-realism, its applicability and its future directions.

This book was conceived in light of our discussions about teaching these ideas to our students and has been written with students and newcomers to ultra-realism in mind. We have tried to break down complex ideas into easily understandable language and use examples to relate these core ideas. As we have taught these ideas to our own students over recent years, we also include some of their insights throughout the book. You will hear their voices and their words in each chapter as they offer insights into how they have come to understand aspects of ultra-realism and provide tips for learning and engaging with each concept. We hope this book helps to make sense of ultra-realism: to do so, we need to start at the beginning and show where ultra-realism comes from and where it sits within the criminological tradition. This is the goal of the next chapter.

2

WHAT IS ULTRA-REALISM?

INTRODUCTION

This chapter will offer a short but comprehensive account of the emergence and development of ultra-realist criminology, its response to mainstream criminology and its core components. If later chapters explore specific components of the theoretical framework, it is important for the reader to situate those elements in the wider whole. The first part of this chapter locates ultra-realist criminology as a response to mainstream criminology and its apparent departure from attempts to understand causation and motivation (Hall, 2012a). We present an ultra-realist critique of established criminological positions through the key question at the heart of ultra-realism: *why do some individuals and groups risk harm to others in the pursuit of their own instrumental and expressive interests?* To answer this question, we present the theoretical and methodological tools provided by ultra-realist criminology and show the varied disciplines and traditions that underpin them. First, we explore critical realism's domains, or layers, of reality and through critique are led into the transcendental materialist framework (Johnston, 2008). In situating the discussion within the thorny issue of structure and agency, this then leads us into an account of the pseudo-pacification process (Hall, 2012a) and the libertine drive of *special liberty* (Hall & Winlow, 2015). Ultra-realism offers a range of tools to answer the key question posed above and, as we argue, suggests that this question should be at the centre of criminological research and investigation. Before we address this further, let us start with an overview of the discipline into which ultra-realism emerged.

CRIMINOLOGICAL ATROPHY: THE STALLED DIALECTIC

Criminology is an ongoing conversation about how and why people transgress the law, patterns of crime over time and what we do about this as a society. A range of perspectives have sought to understand this, and there are a number of assumptions that underpin those viewpoints (Hall, 2012a; Hopkins-Burke, 2018; Ugwudike, 2015). These assumptions reflect criminology's status as an 'importer discipline'; it borrows ideas from philosophy, sociology, psychology and others (Hall & Winlow, 2015). These *domain assumptions* shape the conversation about crime in specific ways:

- How do we measure or identify crime (for example, positivism/empiricism, constructionism)?
- What is true about the world (for example, idealism and realism)?
- Are people inherently good, bad or both (subjectivity)?

Ultra-realist criminology did not emerge in a vacuum; rather, it developed from existing criminological traditions such as left realism (Lea & Young, 1993) and in opposition to the discipline's apparent departure from questions of motivation (Hall & Winlow, 2015). As any first year criminology student can attest, the development of the discipline in the nineteenth and early twentieth century placed great emphasis on understanding the causes of crime: Lombroso's biological positivism situated criminality in one's genetic and physiological make-up; whilst Merton's strain theory contended that *some* individuals who face a disconnect between society's pronouncements of success and attainment and their own means of achievement would turn to crime in order to bridge the gap (Vold, Bernard, & Snipes, 2002). The Chicago School's social ecological perspective believed physical space to be a factor in criminality with a city's 'zone in transition' acting as an incubator of crime, whilst Sutherland's 'differential association' insisted that criminal behaviour was learnt through association with delinquent others (Hopkins-Burke, 2018). These theories differ but all share a common determination to understand the reasons behind those acts we deem to be criminal. However, as the twentieth century progressed and criminology developed as a discipline, that curiosity about *aetiology* – the understanding of causation – diminished and emphasis shifted to questions about what we do with criminals (Hall & Winlow, 2015). Questions about risk management, public protection (Feeley & Simon, 1992) and the control of criminal behaviour, dubbed 'controlology' by Jason Ditton (1979), moved to the fore. Situational crime prevention, underpinned by

Routine Activity Theory (Wilson, 2013), suggested that crime could be managed through the design and control of public space. The strengths and limitations of these perspectives are not central to this book, and we encourage the reader to explore these ideas critically. However, what they lack is a concern about causation and motivation and are instead solely focused on prevention and control.

Additionally, a dominant trend emerged within a 'left idealist' paradigm whereby questions of crime were addressed from the perspective of social constructionism (Hall & Winlow, 2015). The idealist position in philosophy implies that 'reality' as we understand it is limited to what we know about the world, what is mentally constructed by the subject; we can't conceive of a world 'outside' of our sensory perception of it (Tarnas, 2010). In this sense, the world around us is socially constructed. What we experience as 'reality' is, in fact, the result of power relations, interpersonal interactions and socially constructed rules, laws, systems and cultures. This gained prominence following the 1968 uprisings in Europe and the US which signalled a shift, particularly in European social theory and philosophy, away from a focus on material reality (Wolin, 2010). No thinker epitomised this more than Michel Foucault, who argued that society was characterised by power relations that found their basis and legitimacy in socially constructed discourses. Control was established through medical, sexual and penal discourse and diffused throughout the social order (Foucault, 1977). It is impossible to overstate how influential Foucault's thought has been on criminology.

Ultimately, laws and legal systems are reflections of power relations and enforce control on societies and individuals but, crucially, are socially constructed. Labelling theory (Becker, 1997) emerged from symbolic interactionism and argues that the 'deviant', the transgressor of criminal codes, is labelled as such by society and comes to internalise that label and reflect that self-image back through subsequent behaviour. Rather than the subject's actions being harmful or problematic, the socially constructed categories of 'deviant' and 'criminal', and the discourses that reinforce these, come to define the individual. This, crucially, shifts the emphasis away from understanding motivation and focuses instead on power relations, the state and its institutions, and the impact of power and control through socially constructed categories. It also reflects a particular view of human nature, a liberal interpretation of subjectivity as fundamentally 'good' but oppressed by a power imbalance that allows the state to assume deviance and criminality. The focus of criminological research, then, shifts towards highlighting these inequalities, imbalances and harms imposed upon *otherwise good and decent people*. We are not suggesting that the state does not exert power unfairly or that inequalities do not impact on the life chances and choices of people who are inadvertently caught up in the criminal justice process, but this perspective dominates the discipline today and has philosophical underpinnings that, for ultra-realism, are incorrect.

That is not to say that criminology abandoned questions of causation and the reality of crime entirely. Feminist criminology of the 1970s and 1980s offered a vital contribution in shining a critical light on underreported and hidden forms of domestic abuse, sexual violence and other crimes and harms perpetrated against women (Heidensohn, 2012). There are two important aspects of this in relation to ultra-realism: first, feminist criminology proved itself willing to look at and highlight the hidden crimes and harms that mainstream criminology had ignored. As we will see, ultra-realism continues this approach today; second, feminist criminology offers an important corrective to the social constructionist/idealist position that focused on power relations and the imbalances that result in labelling people as criminal. The feminist position highlighted the importance of victims of crime and the impact of violence and abuse. Regardless of debates about whether labelling someone as a violent offender or domestic abuser reflected unequal power relations and the social construction of criminal laws to codify someone as criminal, *their actions had real, material, harmful consequences for victims*. Although ultra-realism diverges from feminist criminology on the theoretical explanations for crime and violence, early feminist criminology represents a key building block for ultra-realism (Hall & Winlow, 2015).

Left and right realism emerged in the 1970s and 1980s as opposing perspectives on the causes and realities of crime, violence and disorder and left realism acts as another foundation for ultra-realism (Hall & Winlow, 2015). In the work of Jock Young, Elliott Currie, John Lea, Roger Matthews and Ian Taylor (Currie, 1985; Lea & Young, 1993; Taylor, Walton, & Young, 2013), left realism acknowledged crimes of the powerful and accepted that criminology did not adequately address this but also asserted, correctly, that most petty crimes were *intra-class*: most crimes committed by working-class people were against other working-class people (Lea & Young, 1993). In offering a mid-range theory of crime (Currie, 1997), left realism connected the micro-level of everyday experiences with the macro-level of state agencies and institutions. The famous 'square of crime' consisted of four relational parts: the victim, the offender, the wider public and the state's institutions. If criminology could understand what was happening at street-level and situate it within a wider context, it could repair the relationship between the four parts of the square and, they theorised, perhaps reduce crime. The crucial role left realism plays for ultra-realism is the acknowledgement that crime and harm take place in complex locales where victims, offenders and the wider community live and that quality of life is impacted by the daily experiences of crime. As we will see, early ultra-realist work (see Hall, Winlow, & Ancrum, 2008; Winlow, 2001) follows the left-realist injunction to look at those problematic locales where crime blights daily existence. By the late 1990s, elements of left realism drifted into a pragmatic 'what works?' focus that corresponded to the New Labour project in the UK. However, this is precisely the point where ultra-realism deviates from left realism:

> *However, the crucial underlying contextual factors of security, decent jobs and housing for all, more fairness and equality, and more cohesive communities – which for early left realists should not be neglected in the way we theorize crime or apply strategies to reduce it – in fact were largely neglected. Repairing relations in the square of crime did little to alleviate the underlying economic and cultural conditions that created and normalized these 'problems'. Left realists helped to pull us out of social constructionist inertia and called for positive interventions, but not at the depth required to promote any real change.*
>
> *(Hall & Winlow, 2015, p. 62)*

Criminology is evidently made up of diverse perspectives that rely on key domain assumptions: ontological, epistemological, ethical and those concerned with the nature of subjectivity. This section has tried to set out some of these positions and show which elements of criminology's history act as the building blocks for ultra-realism. Those perspectives concerned with motivation and the reality of crime, violence and harm are the legacy upon which ultra-realism builds. However, both the social constructionist/idealist position and the empiricism of the positivist tradition have, for ultra-realism, failed to offer a full or accurate explanation for the reality of crime and harm. Therefore, a different philosophical foundation is required and this can initially be found in critical realism, which we turn to next.

CRITICAL REALISM: THE JOURNEY TOWARDS ULTRA-REALISM

As Kotzé (2019, 2021) and Telford (2022) have noted, much of criminological and sociological theorisation rests upon a positivist foundation informed by an empiricist view of science: we collect data and evidence of things seen and counted and develop theoretical explanations and understandings from that baseline. However, this implies that what we can see and count represents *all there is to know about the world* (Winlow & Hall, 2016). This ontological interpretation omits potentially crucial factors that have causative power. Critical realism offers a differentiated or layered ontology – or reality – that accounts for more than the observable. Following the work of Roy Bhaskar (2008), critical realism suggests that reality is made up of three distinct layers:

- Empirical
- Actual
- Real

The empirical represents subjective experiences and observable phenomena. These are our experiences and the things that we can see and count. We can interpret experiences and observations and make sense of the world at this level. The actual represents real events or absences that often sit outside of our everyday experiences but can nevertheless shape subjective experience at the empirical level. The third layer of reality – the real – represents the underlying generative mechanisms that exist beyond sense perception and have a causative effect on the events and experiences at the actual and empirical level. Positivist positions are largely wedded to the empirical layer and, as such, quite often miss what is going on in the other two domains. Indeed, there are enduring properties to mechanisms such as ideology and political economy that we may not be able to see, count and quantify. The critical realist position, supported by ultra-realism, suggests that there is a need for interpretive criminology at the first two levels of reality, but, if analysis stops there, we engage in symptomology instead of getting to the root causative relationships (Hall, 2012a; Hall & Winlow, 2015; Winlow & Hall, 2016). Our analysis only goes so far if it ignores the underlying generative mechanisms at work in society. As an open system, we can't predict that a causal power that we know conceptually exists will exert its influence at any given time – we can say that there is a *probabilistic causal tendency* rather than any universal truth (Hall & Winlow, 2015; Kotzé, 2019; Lloyd, 2018b). The depth realism of the intransitive realm (i.e. beyond experience and observation) must be studied if we are to consider the potential causes of crime and harm and successfully determine the level of intervention required to bring about positive change.

So, ultra-realist criminology looks for evidence of things unseen and asks criminological research to consider the probabilistic causal tendencies associated with depth structures. It pushes analysis beyond the empirical and observable and demands consideration of ideology and political economy. It also implies that there is a reality beyond our own awareness of the world and that this can impact upon our lives, behaviour and decisions; it's not all socially constructed. As Maria suggests in Study-box 1 (see page 18), we need to do more than just glance: we need to really *look* at society and the structures that underpin it. Whilst the enduring properties of political economy, culture and ideology may not be visibly present in criminal acts, patterns of crime or observable harms, they should be part of the analysis. Without consideration of society's depth structures, our knowledge of the world is partial (Kotzé, 2019). Because it looks for probable causal relationships, critical realism and ultra-realism aim to avoid analysis that could be regarded as 'direct expression' theories of crime: the world is too complex a system with too many underlying mechanisms to say that *a* causes *b* or that one thing happens as a direct expression of something else (Raymen & Kuldova, 2021). However, it does create the opportunity to look for probable relationships that can be supported by evidence, analysis and theorisation. As we will see throughout this book, ultra-realism does make claims about the world and about crime, but it does so through correlation and probabilistic causal tendency, rather than clear causation or direct expression. There is, in other words, a clear acknowledgement that individuals can and do act in myriad ways within the structures of any given society.

Critical realism, particularly in Bhaskar's work, also foregrounds the powerful role of absence (Collier, 1994). Much of criminological theory and research is grounded in evidence and data that involve observing, collecting and counting particular phenomena. We often focus on what is there and how that impacts on individuals, groups, institutions and whole societies. How do we know if crime rates are improving or getting worse? We count and quantify the presence of particular offences over time. However, critical realism offers the useful insight that absences can also have probabilistic causal tendencies (Bhaskar, 2008). The absence of a welfare state could have a probabilistic causal impact on poverty and health outcomes. The absence of school during the most restrictive periods of COVID-19 lockdown could have a probabilistic causal impact on educational outcomes and food insecurity (Briggs, Telford, Lloyd, Ellis, & Kotzé, 2021). The absence of stable, well-paid employment opportunities in traditional working-class areas may have a probabilistic causal relationship with certain forms of expressive and instrumental violence (Ellis, 2016; Winlow, 2001). Critical realism and its acknowledgement of the powerful role of absence is significant for ultra-realist criminology and has become a central feature of much of its analysis (Lloyd, 2018b; Winlow & Hall, 2016).

However, while critical realism does offer a powerful and productive alternative to positivist or social constructionist accounts of crime and harm, ultra-realism does not adopt the entire critical realist position. In fact, it departs from it at a crucial juncture. Principally, the split occurs over the nature of subjectivity. Bhaskar argues that the human subject is essentially a positive moral agent (Hall & Winlow, 2015). This suggests that human nature is generally 'good', but those essentially good people can do 'bad' things. Ultra-realism's position, as we will see, draws from Lacan and Johnston to suggest that the subject is non-essential and is neither inherently good nor inherently bad, but instead is capable of both. This moves us towards the core tenets of ultra-realism which we will explore briefly in the remainder of the chapter. We start by picking up this key point about subjectivity – how is the subject neither inherently good nor evil?

THE COMPONENTS OF ULTRA-REALISM

Ultra-realism, generally speaking, suggests that criminology has lost its way. It has moved away from exploring causation and motivation towards administrative and pragmatic 'what works?' research, as well as an idealist belief in social constructions, unequal power relations and stigma. However, there are positives that we need to retain: a focus on the reality of crime, violence and harm in disadvantaged communities, *intra-class* crime as well as crimes of the powerful, and a recognition of the lived reality and experiences of victims. Critical realism provides the tools to consider generative mechanisms and the probabilistic causal tendencies of absence and underlying processes beyond sense perception. Ultra-realism retains these features but also looks to incorporate ideas and thinking from disparate disciplines as well as develop new ideas and concepts of its own. This section picks up from the deviation from critical realism and introduces some of ultra-realism's new concepts. As Hall and Winlow (2012, pp. 8–9) note:

> *We no longer live in the 1960s and whilst we should respect some of the major theoretical accomplishments of the past, we should not slavishly regard this particular period as the pinnacle of human thought and attempt to make its theories fit into a very different political, economic, cultural and ideological climate…(we must) envisage our discipline as both an importer and a generator of cutting-edge ideas relevant to the world today, as well as a meeting place that welcomes lively, cross-disciplinary discussion.*

Some of those new ideas will be explored much more fully in the chapters that follow. In this chapter, we introduce them briefly as ultra-realism's contribution to those challenging but fundamental questions posed in the introduction. For now, let us elucidate further by returning to this important question: why do some people willingly inflict harm on others for their own expressive and/or instrumental ends? Transcendental materialism (Johnston, 2008; Žižek, 2008) suggests that the subject is neither inherently good nor inherently bad but retains the possibility for both, depending upon factors such as ideology, external environment and the unconscious (Hall, 2012b). It offers a different interpretation of subjectivity, not emerging at the point of consciousness, following Descartes, or socially constructed, following Butler, but instead a split-subject characterised by lack (McGowan, 2016). Using the theoretical psychoanalytical framework proposed by Jacques Lacan, transcendental materialism proposes that the subject seeks comfort and coherence in a Symbolic Order – a set of norms, values, codes, signs and symbols that allow us to make sense of the world – which inscribes itself materially through the neuronal receptors in the brain. The subject is hard-wired for plasticity and therefore can change and adapt to external circumstances. The Symbolic Order of any given culture or society, its ideology, codes and norms affect us materially and can be difficult to change. Transcendental materialism's key insight is that people are more malleable and capable of change than ideologies and cultures, and when these linger on past their sell-by-date we encounter what Johnston (2008) refers to as 'deaptation'. The lack at the centre of subjectivity is the motivating force or drive that compels us to act in the world, often in ways that are not rational or clear to the subject. As we will see later, when we begin to apply this to different examples and contexts, it allows different ways of viewing crime, violence, harm and other forms of behaviour.

Ultra-realism has also sought to situate patterns of crime in a much longer historical context. Steve Hall's *pseudo-pacification* process considers how libidinal energy – the drive that emanates from subjective and collective lack – has been transformed and redirected over time in order to facilitate the development of a capitalist political economy. While scholars lauded the 'crime decline' from around the mid-1990s onwards (see Kotzé, 2019), Hall looked backwards and asked why, relatively speaking, societies today were not subject to the same levels of violence, predation and danger that characterised previous periods in human history (Hall, 2012a; Hall & Winlow, 2004). Rather than Norbert Elias' proposal that humanity became more 'civilised' over time, the pseudo-pacification process argues that, over centuries, the libidinal energy that propelled many into violence, bloody feuds, conquest and predatory behaviours was redirected into emerging and nascent market economies (Hall, 2012a). It became easier to trade with strangers if you had confidence that they wouldn't rob or kill you or that your goods could make it to market without routinely being stolen on the road. The process of pseudo-pacification is not straight-forward and requires what Horsley, Kotzé, and Hall (2015) refer to as the 'maintenance of orderly disorder', a balancing act that directs competitive energies into economically useful avenues and away from expressive or instrumental outbursts of disorder and violence. From an ultra-realist perspective, libidinal energy – the drive and desire that characterise lack – exists beneath the surface of society, directed and channelled in various directions but occasionally erupting in problematic ways. An insulating sleeve of social institutions, the welfare state, family ties, community and other mechanisms provides a degree of stability and works to hold those forces in place. However, when this insulating sleeve struggles to contain the mass of libidinal energy, a breakdown in the pseudo-pacification process occurs, resulting in the eruption of various problematic behaviours. As we will explore in more detail later (see Chapter 4), concepts like pseudo-pacification allow us to situate patterns of crime within the context of wider forces.

Relatedly, the concept of *special liberty* offers additional insight to help answer the question of why some people willingly inflict harm on others (Hall, 2012a; Hall & Winlow, 2015). It focuses on individual motivation in the wider context of ideology, environment, unconscious and background but not with the intention of stigmatising the individual. Special liberty reflects a libertine drive whereby the subject, shaped by internal drives and external forces that promote individualism, competition, status and display, sees themself as existing above the herd, above the law and free to act in whatever way furthers their own interests. The subject of special liberty may believe that the rules do not apply to them and that they should be able to do what they want. We can see examples of special liberty in the hard men who dominate council estates, as well as in the politicians who break their own COVID-19 lockdown rules to enjoy parties or carry on extra marital affairs (Briggs et al., 2021). What each of these concepts, and the others that appear in the chapters that follow, has in common is their attempts to make sense of the complex relationship between the individual and the social order in which they exist. This section shows the continuities and divergences present in ultra-realist criminology, what it retains and builds upon as well as some of the new ideas it offers. These concepts attempt to address that key question – why do some people willingly inflict harm upon others in the service of their own expressive and/or instrumental interests? Ultra-realism draws from different disciplines – philosophy, history, neuroscience, psychoanalysis, moral philosophy – in attempts to find answers to this fundamental question and to continue the legacy of criminological theory and its focus on the realities of crime, harm and violence.

CONCLUSION

This chapter has offered a very brief overview of the development of ultra-realist criminology. Many criminological theory modules tend to offer the same potted history of the discipline and often end with left and right realism, cultural criminology or feminist criminology. Some will offer post-colonial criminology or critical race theory. Ultra-realist criminology aims to move the conversation about crime, motivation and causation forward and offer a set of new perspectives that make sense of the world as it is today. It recognises the value of its antecedents and encourages criminologists to retain the useful elements of earlier theories – left realism and feminism are clear examples in terms of their insistence on the reality of crime and harm, its impact on victims and communities and their commitment to shining a light on previously unseen and unheard voices. Ultra-realism also follows the ethnographic tradition of immersing itself in those cultures and communities to gain a rich, deep understanding of the scale of crime, harm and violence. In advocating a return to the discussion of causation, ultra-realism follows critical realism in terms of analysis that indicates probabilistic causal relationships, not direct causation (Winlow & Hall, 2016). Rather than suggesting a direct expression of the relationship between crime and capitalist political economy, ultra-realism's tools – transcendental materialism, pseudo-pacification, special liberty, lack, fetishistic disavowal, etc. – aim to show the complex relationship between individuals, societies and ideologies (Raymen & Kuldova, 2021). In the chapters that follow, we explore these concepts in more detail and hope to demonstrate the value in engaging with these ideas. We start next with transcendental materialism and *Avengers*.

Study-box 1

Student Insight:

Meet Maria, a 46-year-old undergraduate student.

For me, they saved the best till last. Ultra-realism seems scary and technical at first, but don't be afraid to ask questions. As far as the terminology goes, it wasn't so scary once you realise it's all real life and all of us are aware of our surroundings once you take notice. What I would say to anyone is, *do the reading*. I would say this part of the course has been the best for me. As an older person studying this subject, it has been the theory to a life and world I have been living and experiencing for quite some time now. Ultra-realism has helped me to understand the Covid-19 pandemic in lots of respects, politically, financially, culturally, and most of all it has brought to life the real-time experience of the hidden structures and motivations that surround us.

Key Takeaway: My main tip is listen, ask questions and when you look at society, really *look*. Don't just glance as all is not what it seems, what you will learn applies to most of it.

Study Questions:

- In what ways did feminism and left realism influence ultra-realism?
- Can you explain how absences can have probabilistic causal tendencies?
- How does transcendental materialism's interpretation of subjectivity differ from that of critical realism?

Key Reading: Hall, S. and Winlow, S. (2018) 'Ultra-Realism'. In DeKeseredy, W.S. and Dragiewicz, M. (eds) *Routledge Handbook of Critical Criminology*, 2nd Edition, pp. 43-56. London: Routledge.

Fig. 1. Study-Box 1.

3

TRANSCENDENTAL MATERIALISM AND *AVENGERS*

INTRODUCTION

So far, we have presented a fairly basic outline of what ultra-realism is and how it offers an exciting way forward for contemporary criminological theorising, touching upon some of its 'key ingredients' along the way. As we progress through the remaining chapters, we sharpen our focus on some of ultra-realism's core components, beginning here with transcendental materialism. Described as an "ontology of the subject" (Wakeman, 2018, p. 219), this distinctive philosophy provides a unique way to bridge the divide between structure and agency, offering an interesting perspective on just how we become who we are. For criminology, it has exciting potential (Wakeman, 2018) and has been utilised by ultra-realists as a framework for understanding the motivation to inflict harm. For us, transcendental materialism helps to explore and explain the creation of harmful, and indeed criminogenic, subjectivities. To help explain this complex position, we use Marvel's *Avengers* movie series. By exploring the actions and oratories of characters like Loki, Ultron and Thanos, we are able to tease out some of the more intricate components of this philosophy.

DISCLAIMER

Whilst watching the *Avengers* movies, it struck us how vividly some of the characters seemed to capture the essence of the transcendental materialist subject, particularly Loki, Ultron and Thanos. Naturally, we figured they would be a nice fit for this chapter. But, wait. Why are we using non-human characters to explore and explain a theory of *human* subjectivity? True, these antagonists are not human, but there is perhaps some value in acknowledging that "the truth of humanity lies in the inhuman" (Eagleton, 2009, p. 281). Indeed, it is our contention that Loki, Ultron and Thanos represent hyper-idealised transcendental materialist subjects. Through their exacerbated actioning of neoliberal ideological tenets, they do not appear different from us, so much as they are *more human than us*. If we calibrate our theoretical lens to peer more deeply, we can see that their ostensible otherness is overridden by sameness in the order of values, drives and desires (Hall, 2012a). Whilst they may exhibit an exacerbated extrapolation of our present norms, values and subjectivities, they do not depart from them (Raymen, 2018). Let us be clear here: we are not suggesting that there is a direct equivalence between these antagonists and human subjects. Rather, we maintain that their exacerbated exhibitions of transcendental materialist qualities apropos human subjectivity provide a more nuanced and sharply focused lens through which to analyse subjectivity. Accordingly, we consider it appropriate, if not advantageous, to demonstrate this model of subjectivity through these antagonists who demonstrate its complexity so vividly.

A NEW THEORY OF SUBJECTIVITY

If transcendental materialism is best described as an ontology of the subject, we need to get to grips with what these terms mean if we are to make sense of this philosophy. The 'subject' is you, your friends and your parents; it is a person of a particular social, economic, cultural and political space or setting. Ontology refers to the essence of being, "what human beings and their natural and social worlds actually are" (Hall & Winlow, 2015, p. 98). So, by drawing on philosophy, psychoanalysis and contemporary developments in neuroscience, transcendental materialism endeavours to explain the relationship between the individual subject and the wider sociosymbolic structure (Hall & Winlow, 2015). Its starting point is the idea that the subject is non-essential, neither good nor evil, yet exists with the inherent potential to be either (Hall & Winlow, 2015; Johnston, 2008). Acknowledging our biological origins, transcendental materialism suggests that the human brain is hard-wired for plasticity (Hall, 2012a). The brain's materiality, its neuronal receptors, can break down and reconstitute which allows the individual to adapt and survive in various environments (Johnston & Malabou, 2013; Wakeman, 2018).

From this biological starting point, we can begin to consider the relationship between the material subject and the wider social order.

Human subjectivity, our *beingness*, arises from this material starting point, the human brain, but exists as more than simply our material grounding; it can transcend material origins in a way that prevents being reduced to simple materiality. As the subject acts in the world and engages with the external environment, that external stimulus *feeds back* into the material core, fundamentally changing it at a material level (Lloyd, 2018b). As we absorb the external environment around us, it has a material consequence for our very being. Crucially, this is not a one-way street. Instead, as we act in the world, we can mould or shape the world too. These changes, in turn, feed back into the human brain and continue to shape our subjectivity. So, the relationship between subject and environment is important. But how exactly does this relationship play out? For this, transcendental materialism draws upon a Lacanian-Žižekian framework that charts the interplay between three registers of reality: the Real, the Imaginary, and the Symbolic Order (Žižek, 2008).

The Real represents a traumatic, unrealisable excess; something beyond symbolisation that we can be aware of but not find the words to describe. The subjective trauma of confronting the Real propels us into the warm embrace of the dominant Symbolic Order; the signs, values, norms, codes, language and ideology that shape and present 'reality' around us (Žižek, 2006). The Symbolic Order allows us to make sense of the world we live in and forestalls a confrontation with the Real. Now, rather than being forced into the Symbolic Order by some external force, the subject *actively solicits* its inclusion at an unconscious level (Hall, 2012a, 2012d; Johnston, 2008). This active solicitation involves a process of 'denaturalisation' whereby we pass from a raw state of nature to a recognisable state of culture within which the attendant values, norms and practices are re-naturalised in the subject's neurological circuitry and accepted as timeless facts of life (Kotzé, 2019; Winlow & Hall, 2013).

The upshot is that these cultural reference points limit the horizons of possibility because a Symbolic Order generates the subjectivities it needs and requires. This does not mean that we are not free to make choices, but that our choices are rather constrained. Remember that the plasticity of the human brain means that the subject is sculpted by experience (Johnston, 2008); as we act in the world, the world feeds back onto our material being. So, if a Symbolic Order is benevolent, generous, caring and collective, it will generate appropriate subjectivities. If a Symbolic Order is characterised by competition, status, individualism and self-interest, it will generate subjectivities accordingly (Lloyd, 2018b). Today's dominant Symbolic Order is neoliberal consumer capitalism and it is characterised by individualism, competition, opportunity, the pursuit of self-interest and liberal conceptions of freedom (Milbank & Pabst, 2018). Accordingly, the transcendental materialist framework indicates that subjectivities are constituted along these lines. Do not make the mistake of thinking that this is reductionist; we still retain the agency to act and make our own decisions and therefore change or shape the social and cultural environment we inhabit. Rather than directly determining subjectivity, the Symbolic Order's norms, values and dispositions make it more *likely* that subjects will embody corresponding characteristics.

While the subject demonstrates an inherent plasticity and flexibility in adapting to changing circumstances, the Symbolic Order struggles with change and adaptation (Hall, 2012d). When a Symbolic Order, or ideological framework, persists long after the material conditions that created it have gone, it becomes counter-productive or even harmful. Johnston (2008, p. 175) refers to this process as "deaptation". Despite no longer being able to successfully integrate the majority of the populace within its master-narrative, neoliberal consumer capitalism lingers on well past its sell-by-date and continues to exert its influence over our lives, often with harmful consequences (Kotzé, 2019). Indeed, evidence is beginning to mount of the increasingly deapted nature of neoliberalism and its manifest criminogenic and zemiogenic conditions. Having bought into a deapted Symbolic Order, more and more people experience extreme poverty, precarity, various forms of violence and innumerable antagonisms as we all pursue our own self-interests (Briggs & Gamero, 2017; Ellis, 2016; Horsley & Lloyd, 2020). Transcendental materialism is certainly a tricky subject to grasp, so let's see if we can make things a little clearer with the help of some pop-culture.

ENTER THE AVENGERS

Through a doorway opened by the Tesseract, Loki, the adopted son of Odin from Asgard, appears on Earth in a flash of blue cosmic light. He wastes no time in dispatching the small security force that confronts him before declaring that he comes "with glad tidings, of a world made free". With warranted concern, the Director of *S.H.I.E.L.D*, Nick Fury, asks the intruder from what we are being freed? "Freedom. Freedom is life's great lie, once you accept that, in your heart, you will know peace", retorts Loki. In what way can freedom be a lie? For us, Loki is perhaps tacitly referring to the loss of the big Other, the communal network of social institutions, customs and laws to which individuals are socialised (Myers, 2003; Winlow & Hall, 2013). Now, the big

Other never really existed as a material 'thing', it was more like a collective fib where we all acted *as if* we believed in its unwritten constitution. It *became* real because people acted *as if it was real* (Kotzé, 2019). So where did it go? Myers (2003) notes that the death of the big Other was perpetrated by the reflexivity of liberal-postmodernism. We no longer accept basic truths or believe in any adjudicating authority and have lost faith in social institutions and conventions (Winlow & Hall, 2013).

Under the guise of liberal-postmodernism, we now occupy a terrain where the 'self' constitutes "the ultimate horizon of meaning" (Žižek, 2006, p. 10). However, having been set 'free' from the constraints of the big Other, we "have also been untethered from any sense of fixity, stability or a means of making coherent sense of our world" (Raymen, 2016, p. 508). What Loki identifies as 'life's great lie' is actually the paradox of postmodernism – the 'freedom' afforded to us by the death of the big Other is actually a burden which manifests in a desire for discipline as less and less of the world around us makes sense (Myers, 2003; Winlow & Hall, 2013). Devoid of shared elements of social knowledge, understanding and agreement, there is only interminable disagreements and dilemmas (Raymen, 2019a), and Loki calls us out on it:

> *Kneel before me! Is not this simpler? Is this not your natural state? It's the unspoken truth of humanity that you crave subjugation, the bright lure of freedom diminishes your life's joy in a mad scramble for power, for identity; you were made to be ruled.*

In these uncomfortable words, Loki dismantles liberal-postmodernism's interpretation of freedom and identifies the stresses of simultaneously trying to fit in and stand out in the realm of consumer symbolism (Hall, Winlow, & Ancrum, 2008). Similarly, he alludes to the process of subjectivisation, or what Hall (2012d) aptly terms 'the solicitation of the trap'. Remember that we are not forced by some external power into the dominant Symbolic Order but *actively solicit* it. The attendant norms, values and practices are then re-naturalised in our neurological circuitry influencing and restricting our behaviour, and so sociosymbolic systems can be constraining rather than liberating (Winlow & Hall, 2013). In many ways, the detached 'freedom' we now experience is oppressive and instead of constituting some sort of gain, it is unconsciously experienced as an acute loss, intensifying the sense of lack at the core of our very being (Raymen, 2019b). Nevertheless, despite its severely deapted nature, we continue to participate in, and help reproduce, a sociosymbolic order that produces inordinate social harms (Kotzé, 2019, 2020).

Whilst Loki draws attention to our solicitation of the trap, it is Ultron, in the second *Avengers* movie, who most clearly demonstrates this subjectivisation process. In what is a relatively short cinematic sequence we see Ultron pass from a raw state of nature where un-symbolised stimuli irrupt upon the senses to a recognisable state of culture. In the beginning of the sequence, Ultron is confused as his prematurational being occupies a place in the Real, devoid of symbolisation, or any visual cues at all as he first establishes consciousness. "This feels weird, this feels wrong", he says questioningly. From here, Ultron endeavours to escape from the Real by actively soliciting the dominant sociosymbolic order, in this case the subroutines and programming designed by Tony Stark. This helps him make sense of the world he has entered, realising he is "a peacekeeping programme; created to help the Avengers". However, he quickly realises that he has solicited a trap as the sociosymbolic order's deaptation becomes evident, illustrated by the flashing images of humanity's destructive failure. "I don't get it, the mission" he says as Jarvis offers his assistance to what appears to be a malfunctioning Ultron. Subsequently, he embarks on a mission to resolve the issue of deaptation – albeit with an extreme sense of special liberty (see Chapter 4) and a willingness to inflict harm on others.

From a transcendental materialist perspective, what Ultron is essentially pursuing is the creation of a new Symbolic Oder. Seemingly aware of the durable yet dysfunctional rigidity of the dominant Symbolic Order, he contends that humanity's 'evolution' to a more peaceful society is negated by our commitment to a deapted socio-economic system and the harmful conditions it fosters:

> *I'm sorry, I know you mean well you just didn't think it through. You want to protect the world but you don't want it to change. How is humanity saved if it's not allowed to evolve?*

Ultron also quite rightly identifies our tendency to pay lip-service to a desire to change the world for the better whilst simultaneously engaging in a range of false activities that only serve to ensure that no change will actually occur (see Kotzé, 2020). Indeed, as we demonstrate in Chapter 6, we are, for the most part, content with providing the appearance of change precisely so that nothing has to change (Winlow, 2013). This may be because real change necessitates that we walk the difficult road back through the indeterminacy of our material being on the road to creating a new Symbolic Order (Winlow & Hall, 2013). Accordingly, as Ultron points out, the power to make real change terrifies us and so we are reluctant to try (see also Hall & Winlow, 2018b).

Therefore, despite having a malleable material basis capable of adaptation, we are ideologically committed to sociosymbolic inertia.

The relationship between the subject and the sociosymbolic structure within which one resides is clearly complex. However, by exploring this complex relationship, we can begin to better understand how harmful subjectivities are produced (Raymen, 2016). Here, Thanos, who we are introduced to in the third and fourth films, provides another opportunity to try and unpick this. Recall how subjectivities are generated in line with the contexts of the dominant sociosymbolic order (Lloyd, 2018b), well, this is demonstrated in *Infinity War* when Thanos recounts the destruction of Titan:

> *Titan was like most planets, too many mouths and not enough to go around. And when we faced extinction, I offered a solution [Genocide? – Dr Strange]. At random, dispassionate, fair, rich and poor alike... And what I predicted came to pass. With all six stones I could simply snap my fingers, they would all cease to exist and I call that, mercy.*

Here we see that Thanos' violent subjectivity is intimately connected to the context of his planet's impending doom; the ultimate culmination of its deaptation. The change he undergoes, as he becomes genocidal, is rooted in the interactions between the desperate situation of the world he occupies and the plasticity of the brain's synapses that his subjectivity emerges out of. As Wakeman (2018: 220, original emphasis) puts it in relation to Walter White in *Breaking Bad*, "as he sees, thinks, desires, fears and does, *so he slowly but surely becomes*". Accordingly, the subject undergoes a process of *becoming* as they interact with the external environment which subsequently feeds back onto their neuronal receptors, altering the material composition of the subject (Lloyd, 2018b). We can see a similar process of *becoming* across the first three *Pirates of the Caribbean* films.

Ms Elizabeth Swann, daughter of Governor Weatherby Swann, plays a key role throughout the *Pirates of the Caribbean* story line. Very early on in *The Curse of the Black Pearl,* we see traces of young Ms Swann's sense of adventure, but this is overlaid with the reserved decorum and propriety associated with her class. As the story develops, we see the tension between these states of being ebb and flow. However, during the second and third films, we see Elizabeth change. The more she is enmeshed within the treacherous and violent world of the pirates, the more she slowly but surely becomes more pirate-like; to the extent that she actually *becomes* the pirate King in the third film. We can see this transformation play out on screen. From the relatively timid Governor's daughter, who requests parley in the first film, Elizabeth goes on to use the threat of violence to acquire a letter of marque for Will Turner in the second. By the third film, she has become proficient in, and more than willing to use, physical violence as demonstrated early on by her seizing of Tai Huang at knife point.

This transformation is gradual and demonstrates that the "non-essential subject is shaped by the material reality of the world in which one lives" (Lloyd, 2018b, p. 29). What makes Elizabeth Swann a particularly good example is that she also demonstrates how the subjectivisation process is not one-directional. Yes, she adapts to external circumstances at a material level, but she also acts in the world, shaping and influencing it, and as she does so, those changes exert experiential feedback that alters her subjectivity (Kotzé, 2019; Lloyd, 2018b). In both cases, then, we can see that Thanos and Elizabeth *become* violent as a result of a complex interplay between the subject and the wider sociosymbolic order within which they are enmeshed. However, Raymen (2018) suggests that a process of *reversion* is at play in the production of harmful and/or violent subjectivities. Here the subject reverts back to a more ruthless and unmitigated set of behavioural codes associated with a previous age (see Chapter 4). This reversion releases the subject from the social order's ethico-social constraints (Raymen, 2018), allowing them to act out a range of stimulated drives and desires unconstrained by regulatory forces. This also seems to hold true for our examples as a gradual erosion of ethico-legal constraints is evident in the transformation of Elizabeth Swann, whilst for Thanos, such constraints have disappeared entirely allowing him to enact his devastating 'solution'.

Rather than viewing harmful and/or violent subjectivities as being the product of either *becoming* or *reversion*, we suggest that *both* forces are at play. Within the context of neoliberal consumer capitalism, becoming and reversion exist in a complex reciprocal relationship with each force acting upon the other to produce subjectivities capable of inflicting severe harms. We will return to this theoretical development in Chapter 9, but for now, it is worth us clarifying the link to criminogenesis. In the first instance, recall how in order to escape the trauma of the Real, where un-symbolised stimuli irrupt upon the senses, we actively solicit inclusion within the dominant Symbolic Order. Once incorporated, the attendant values, norms and practices are inscribed on our neurological circuitry, influencing and restricting behaviour accordingly (Hall, 2012d). We have already seen that if the Symbolic Order is benevolent, generous, caring and collective, then it will generate subjectivities along these lines. However, what happens if the Symbolic Order into which the subject enters is deapted and characterised by competitive individualism, self-interest, greed and envy? Put simply, the subject is likely to act in ways that reflect these characteristics, with potentially harmful consequences.

Remember, this is not a deterministic one-way street. The subject has the agency to act in the world, shape it and influence it, but in today's world, such actions are more than likely to be influenced and restricted by the negative ideology of capitalist realism (Fisher, 2009). So, the upshot is that we have actively solicited inclusion within a deapted Symbolic Order likely to cultivate subjectivities susceptible to criminogenesis (Kotzé, 2019). Indeed, it is clear to see that neoliberal consumer capitalism produces severe criminogenic consequences, inequality, anxiety, socio-economic instability and insecurity, competitive individualism and a willingness to inflict harm on others. Each of these has the *potential* to foster criminal responses in attempts to ameliorate and/or hyper-conform to them (Kotzé, 2019). In many ways, this is what the antagonists in *Avengers* demonstrate.

All three of them endeavour to ameliorate an issue: for Loki, it is the paradox of postmodernism, whilst for Ultron and Thanos, it was the issue of deaptation. However, in attempting to address these issues, they all exhibit the same core energies, drives and desires that reside at the heart of the neoliberal subject as they bypass morality and social obligations to *simply act* to secure success in the dominant sociosymbolic order (Hall, 2015). Therefore, whilst they identify the transcendental materialist subject and the flaws within our current sociosymbolic order, they also exhibit exacerbated traces of this very subjectivity. In fact, through their extreme actioning of some of neoliberalism's more destructive tenets that have come to occupy the centre stage of our social order (Raymen, 2016), Loki, Ultron and Thanos perhaps represent hyper-idealised transcendental materialist subjects.

CONCLUSION

Ultra-realist criminology has spearheaded some of the most promising theoretical developments in the discipline's history (Wakeman, 2018). The criminological extrapolation of transcendental materialism has been crucial in this regard, serving as a cornerstone of the ultra-realist framework. As a philosophy of the subject, transcendental materialism demonstrates how subjectivity emerges out of a material base but then becomes enmeshed in the social and cultural context one is located in (Wakeman, 2018). Environmental stimulus feeds back onto the subject's neuronal receptors as one interacts with the world, shaping the material composition of the subject. This means that as non-essential subjects, we are literally shaped by the material reality of the world in which we live, but we can also act in the world to shape and influence it with those changes subsequently feeding back into the human brain, continuously shaping our subjectivity (Lloyd, 2018b).

From a criminological perspective, if we are able to grasp the complex relationship between subject and environment, then we can better understand how harmful subjectivities are formed. For example, by positioning Thanos and Elizabeth Swann as transcendental materialist subjects, we were able to demonstrate how they *became* violent as a result of a complex interplay between the subject and the context of the wider sociosymbolic order within which they are enmeshed. However, it is important to remember that the process of *reversion* also plays a key role here in the production of harmful subjectivities. By releasing the subject from the social order's ethico-social constraints, one is free to act out a range of stimulated drives and desires unconstrained by regulatory forces (Raymen, 2018). So, if subjectivities are generated in accordance with the character of the dominant Symbolic Order, what, then, is the condition of ours? Unfortunately, the diagnosis is not good. We currently occupy a severely deapted sociosymbolic order that produces a highly criminogenic and zemiogenic social context. Whilst it is not inevitable that individuals absorbed into a Symbolic Order that cultivates such contexts will inflict harm onto others, it is certainly more *likely*. Indeed, ultra-realism does not deal in deterministic absolutes; instead it identifies probabilistic causal tendencies (Hall & Winlow, 2015).

As this chapter has no doubt demonstrated, transcendental materialism is an important but tricky position to get to grips with. Sometimes the best way to grasp something this complex is to break it down into manageable chunks. So, for example, before trying to make sense of the three registers of reality, try to understand how the human brain is hard-wired for plasticity and how subjectivity emerges out of a material base but becomes more-than-material as we interact with our surroundings. Just take it one step at a time. Previous work by Wakeman (2018) and Raymen (2018) demonstrates how useful pop-culture can be in helping to grasp complex theoretical ideas. So, why not have a go yourself? Now that we have outlined the core elements of transcendental materialism, you could perhaps use the expansive Marvel cinematic universe, which plays host to a range of characters across the original comic books, Hollywood movies and television series to try to identify and think through some of these elements. Remember, as Nicola points out in Study-box 2, this is complex material, so try not to worry if you don't quite get it straight away (Study-box 2 (see page 29)).

Study-box 2

Student Insight:

Meet Nicola, a 38-year-old undergraduate student.

Try not to worry if you do not grasp the content straightaway, it is to be expected, it is complex. Preparation and further reading are a must to help understand this subject. Personally, for me it took quite some time. However, I found reading around the subject before attending lectures really helped. For instance, when learning about transcendental materialism I found it a little overwhelming, but by reading around the subject before the lecture, even if I didn't understand much, I could slot certain bits into place by the time the lecture had finished. Also, by reading and planning beforehand I was able to prepare questions I would like to ask. Reading and preparing questions meant I could obtain as much as possible from the lecture. Once the various components come together, they can be related to many aspects of things that occur within society.

Key Takeaway: Try not to get frustrated. An understanding will happen, almost like the flick of a switch.

Study Questions:

- Try to explain why the subjectivisation process is not one-directional.
- What is deaptation and how can it be harmful or even criminogenic?
- What role does the process of *reversion* play in the production of harmful subjectivities?

Key Reading: Wakeman, S. (2018) 'The One Who Knocks and the One Who Waits: Gendered Violence in *Breaking Bad*', *Crime, Media, Culture,* 14 (2), pp. 213-228.

Fig. 2. Study-Box 2.

4

PSEUDO-PACIFICATION, SPECIAL LIBERTY AND *PIRATES OF THE CARIBBEAN*

INTRODUCTION

As demonstrated in the previous chapter, harmful subjectivities may be considered a product of a severely deapted sociosymbolic order. Arguably, the more individuals become absorbed into a Symbolic Order that cultivates competitive individualism, envy, narcissism, immediate gratification and an unwavering sense of entitlement, the more *likely* it is that they will risk harm to others in order to achieve their own self-interest. But how did we arrive at a point where these harmful tenets are seemingly stitched into the very fabric of social life itself? This chapter will attempt to answer this very question by exploring the ultra-realist concept of the pseudo-pacification process. Originally devised by Steve Hall (2000, *passim*), this cultural-historical theory explains how harm, and violence in particular, are not aberrations of the capitalist system. Rather, they are "integrated in the system's dynamic core and reproduced in its conventional culture and subjectivity" (Hall, 2015, p. 130). To help us explain this complex perspective, we draw upon the *Pirates of the Caribbean* film series; reference is also made to the *Indiana Jones* films.

A BACKGROUND TO FAKING CIVILITY

Hall (2002) points out that liberal-capitalism has a complex relationship with violence. Evidence suggests that the emergence of the capitalist project coincided with a decline in extreme forms of arbitrary interpersonal violence. Beginning in England from around the late fourteenth century, a similar trend occurred in other capitalist nations over different timescales (Hall & Winlow, 2015). For some, this decline could be attributed to a 'civilising process' (Elias, 2000). Characterised by a series of complex and interlocking psycho-social transformations (Horsley, Kotzé, & Hall, 2015), this process can perhaps be best understood by highlighting its key phases. First was the state's monopolisation of violence. Instead of individuals needing to perpetrate personal violence in defence of honour and property, the state offered legal protections and eliminated the public entitlement to physical violence (Ellis, 2019). This created the context within which stable social interdependencies could be created and maintained. Put simply, this means that individuals gradually learned to value and empathise with each other (Hall, 2007). Over time, these behavioural shifts were reproduced by the cultural diffusion of social etiquette throughout the social body as 'manners' permeated into everyday culture (Ellis, 2019; Horsley et al., 2015). The upshot was that individuals were said to have developed a revulsion towards violence, and it was no longer approved as a means of resolving personal disputes (Hall, 2012a).

As insightful as Elias's theory is, there are several issues with it. Space precludes a thorough analysis of these here (see Horsley et al., 2015), but suffice to say that capitalism has *never* been a civilising process. Rather, it is more accurate to describe it as a *pseudo-pacification process* (Hall, 2015). Indeed, Hall and Winlow (2004) point out that the development of repugnance towards violence and the reduction of interpersonal hostility was not driven by an attempt to 'civilise' and 'stabilise' for their own sakes. Instead, they were simply historical by-products of the economic need for pacification in an emerging market economy (Hall & Winlow, 2015). The proto-capitalists realised that a market economy cannot thrive under conditions of extreme and arbitrary physical violence. If the distribution of money and commodities were to prevail, then the right to property needed to be protected and violent interactions attenuated as much as possible (Hall & Winlow, 2015). We can see this initial logic played out in both *Dead Man's Chest* and *Salazar's Revenge*. In the latter, we are introduced to Armando Salazar, a high-ranking officer in the Spanish Navy who relentlessly hunts pirates. Whilst not made explicit in the film, we could infer that his duties were, at least in part, in keeping with the need to protect vulnerable transport ships carrying vast quantities of gold and silver from the New World as Spain amassed a vast fortune during a time when the oceans of the world were divided between Spain and Portugal (Haywood & Spivak, 2012).

Similarly, in *Dead Man's Chest,* we are introduced to Lord Cutler Beckett of the East India Trading Company. In his bid to secure trade and capitalise on opportunities to dominate the market, he certainly embodied the favoured tradition of East India traders: "trade where necessary and plunder where possible" (Robins, 2012, p. 45). This entrepreneurial imperative frames Beckett's pursuit of Davy Jones' chest: "Beckett wants the compass. Only one reason for that" (Gibbs). "Of course, he wants the chest" (Sparrow). "If the Company controls the chest, they control the sea…and bad, bad for every mother's son what calls himself pirate" (Gibbs).

It was not simply the elimination of interpersonal violence that the proto-capitalists needed to contend with. They also acknowledged that social conditions built on ethico-legal regulation and institutionalised altruism hampered the market's expansion (Hall, 2015; Kotzé, 2019). Again, we see this play out in dialogue between Beckett and Ms Swann: "No doubt you've discovered that loyalty is no longer the currency of the realm as your father believes" (Beckett). "Then what is?" (Ms Swann) "I'm afraid that currency is the currency of the realm" (Beckett). Accordingly, these two extremes needed truncating to create a third space that exists somewhere between pacified order and violent disorder; a kind of 'orderly disorder' (Horsley et al., 2015). The fundamental purpose of this space is to tap into and harness the dynamic force generated by the tension between stimulation and pacification – the two poles of the pseudo-pacification process.

STIMULATION AND PACIFICATION

The function of the pseudo-pacification process is easy enough to understand; it secures the expansion of the capitalist market economy by stimulating and harnessing the drives and desires of the populace (Hall, 2002). *How* it does this is a bit more complex. Recall how arbitrary physical violence needed to be evacuated from social life. This violent energy did not simply vanish; rather, it was 'repurposed' into the psycho-social fuel that powers the market (Kotzé, 2019). At the heart of the pseudo-pacification process lies a converter that sublimates violent thymotic energies into highly aggressive but physically non-violent forms of sociosymbolic competition (Raymen, 2018). To fully grasp this conversion process, we need to have some understanding of the dimorphic nature of violence (Hall, 2000). Put simply, this means that violence exists in both physical and symbolic forms and the pseudo-pacification process works to transform the former into the latter.

However, we should emphasise that this should not be understood as a simple 'hydraulic process'. The conversion process opens up new zones of approval and possibility in the realm of sociosymbolic competition but does not *determine* that symbolic forms of violence will seamlessly replace physical forms. We must remember that whilst action is a product of agency, this process opens up economic spaces structured by laws and cultural norms where agency is limited in some ways and encouraged in others. In short, it shifts the *probability* of action towards pseudo-pacified competition. Although, as we shall see later in the chapter, the pseudo-pacification process does not work perfectly, some individuals still resort to physical violence. Nevertheless, what this highlights is how the process tries to manipulate the dimorphic nature of violence.

To help clarify this a bit more, we draw on Žižek (2009) who distinguishes between *subjective* and *objective* violence. The former refers to physical violence perpetrated by an identifiable agent, whilst the latter refers to violent acts that are far less visible. Subsumed under the heading of objective violence, there exists two sub-sets which Žižek refers to as *symbolic* and *systemic*. The former refers to violence embodied in language, such as sexist or racist slurs, for example. The latter refers to violence that is "inherent in the social conditions of global capitalism" that cause things like unemployment, homelessness and poverty (Žižek, 2009, p. 12). Far from constituting some disturbance to the 'normal' state of things, systemic violence is actually the consequence of the *smooth functioning* of the liberal-capitalist system.

Against this backdrop, then, we can begin to understand that the pressure exerted to eliminate physical violence from public life energised a sublimation process that converts subjective violence into objective violence (Hall, Winlow, & Ancrum, 2008). Rather than acting as a 'civilising' agent, the democratisation of objective violence gives individuals licence to compete against each other with greater intensity. The core energies stimulated by liberal-capitalism – greed, envy, competitive individualism, anxiety, opportunism and ruthless ambition – are therefore simultaneously stimulated and pacified, and then harnessed to energise the market economy (Hall, 2013; Kotzé, 2019). Held in undialectical tension, these two forces constitute the dynamic yet fragile pseudo-pacification process (Hall, 2013).

Helping to further illustrate the point, Hall (2012a) likens the whole process to an electrical wire carrying a powerful current. The copper wiring constitutes the aforementioned stimulated drives associated with liberal-capitalism, whilst the fabric or plastic outer layer forms the insulating sleeve of ethical-legal restraints that keep the aggressive current from causing too much damage. Similarly, we could refer to the internal wiring carrying the current as the generative core of capitalism whilst the outer covering functions like a regulatory jacket (Lloyd, 2018a). Using this latter analogy, we can illustrate this further by referring to the *Indiana Jones* films. In this classic film franchise, there are two sides to the protagonist that we think embody the pseudo-pacification process. On the one hand, Indiana Jones personifies the generative core of liberal-capitalism as he keenly competes for "fortune and glory, kid". In doing so, he often breaks various legal codes – what Hall and Winlow (2015) refer to as the technical laws of capitalism – and even gets labelled a grave robber rather than an archaeologist. On the other hand, we see Dr Jones personifying the regulatory jacket as an ethical-legal restraint that prevents him from simply looting graves and selling treasures on the black market, like Belloq in *Raiders of the Lost Ark*. "That belongs in a museum", exclaims Dr Jones about the Cross of Coronado. In this way, we can see the undialectical tension between the simultaneous stimulation and pacification of ambition, competition and status being played out on screen.

SPECIAL LIBERTY

What *Indiana Jones* and *Pirates of the Caribbean* demonstrate particularly well is the tension between capitalism's technical and symbolic laws. As alluded to earlier, the technical laws of capitalism are simply the prohibited norms encapsulated in legal codes. These "function to prevent the subjective drives and desires the system incites from overheating and collapsing social life into [subjectively] violent competition" (Hall & Winlow, 2015, p. 114). Conversely, the symbolic law of capitalism is neatly encapsulated in its ruling ideology: "grab what you can, look out for 'number one' and transform the self into a winner" (Treadwell, Briggs, Winlow, & Hall, 2013, p. 14). In *The Curse of the Black Pearl*, this central tenet is enthusiastically toasted by Sparrow and Gibbs in one of Tortuga's taverns: "Take what you can!" (Sparrow). "Give nothing back!" (Gibbs) – and is repeated, this time with Gibbs taking the lead, at the end of the third film. In relation to the pseudo-pacification process, this represents the liberation and democratisation of drives that both fuel interpersonal competition and normalise violent subjectivities (Ellis, 2019).

Rather than cutting against the grain of capitalism, most acquisitive and non-political forms of crime actually observe capitalism's symbolic law (Hall & Winlow, 2015). This is usually aided by a healthy dose of what Hall (2012a) calls 'special liberty'. Put simply, this is an anti-ethos that emboldens individuals to simply act towards the fulfilment of their own interests regardless of the harm it may cause to others. It provides individuals with a sense of entitlement to do whatever is necessary to further their own instrumental and/or expressive interests, whether that be in the realms of business or pleasure (Hall & Winlow, 2015; Winlow & Hall, 2019). Jack Sparrow certainly demonstrates his commitment to capitalism's symbolic law and exercise of special liberty when he is questioned by Murtogg and Mullroy at the docks in Port Royal:

> *Alright then, I confess. It is my intention to commandeer one of these ships, pick up a crew in Tortuga, raid, pillage and plunder and otherwise pilfer my weaselly black guts out.*

What makes Sparrow's confession even more interesting is that it demonstrates an *over-identification* with, and *hyper-conformity* to, the core tenets of liberal-capitalism. Free from ethico-social constraints, he exercises the "thymotic human drives and energies that have been harnessed for the advancement of capitalist economies throughout history" (Raymen, 2018, p. 436).

The conviction that one is entitled to simply act in accordance to one's drives and desires regardless of how harmful they might be does not belong to some 'othered' criminal class. Rather, it is a general cultural current – "a condensation of the dark side of liberal individualism" (Hall & Wilson, 2014, p. 645) – and is frequently exercised by business operators to inflict harms on people, communities and the environment in the name of progress and prosperity (Hall, 2015). Indeed, this is demonstrated by Lord Cutler Beckett throughout *Dead Man's Chest* and *At World's End*. In his endeavour to simply 'get things done' in service of the Company, we see Beckett extort the Governor to acquire his authority, his influence in London and his loyalty to the East India Trading Company. Once the Governor yields to Beckett's demands, we see his commitment to the logic of the market further demonstrated when he says to Mercer, "every man has a price he will willingly accept, even for what he hopes never to sell". Again, in the name of wealth creation, Beckett bypasses socio-ethical norms as he prepares to eliminate Sparrow: "it's nothing personal Jack, it's just good business".

What we see throughout the *Pirates of the Caribbean* films, then, is a core facet of entrepreneurial criminality played out on screen; competitive individualism, aggressive instrumentalism and the use of violence in the name of 'getting things done' regardless of the harm caused (Raymen, 2018). Many of the leading characters imagine themselves in possession of a personalised state of exception which grants them subjective permission to risk harm to others in pursuit of their own instrumental and/or expressive self-interests. This is comedically expressed quite well by the seemingly dim-witted Ragetti in *Dead Man's Chest*:

> *Well, each wants the chest for himself, don't he? Mr Norrington I think is trying to regain a bit of honour, old Jack's looking to trade it, save his own skin, and Turner there, I think he's trying to settle some unresolved business betwixt him and his twice cursed pirate father.*

Together, special liberty and the broader pseudo-pacification process form a powerful macro-cultural current that underlies liberal-capitalism (Hall & Wilson, 2014). The result, as demonstrated throughout the films discussed here, is not fully civilised individuals, but pseudo-pacified subjects characterised by intensely competitive drives and desires who do not reject violence but mobilise its dimorphic nature in specific ways for specific purposes (Hall, 2020). In this way, as the culture laid down by the pseudo-pacification process developed and diffused throughout the social body (Hall, 2020), capitalism has been able to create ideal-type subjects capable of driving economic expansion by acting out their competitive drives and desires and, where necessary, inflicting harm on others in pursuit of them (Kotzé, 2019).

In general terms, the pseudo-pacification process works in a dynamic yet undialectical way to stimulate the libidinal forces of ambition, competition, envy and narcissism whilst at the same time pacifying this violent energy to ensure it remains economically functional (Horsley et al., 2015). In other words, whilst the process generally discourages outbursts of subjective violence, it actually encourages socially destructive forms of objective violence so as to intensify sociosymbolic competition. Social solidarity is therefore crushed under the weight of competitive individualism as individuals ruthlessly compete in aggressive but physically non-violent ways for distinction, status and symbols of success. Over the past four decades, this has intensified (Raymen, 2016), resulting in the breakdown of the pseudo-pacification process.

THE BREAKDOWN OF THE PSEUDO-PACIFICATION PROCESS

Slowly but surely the generative core of capitalism is stimulating more energy than the regulatory jacket is capable of pacifying. To use our previous analogy, the outer covering of our wire has become incredibly worn and thin. The powerful current is now more likely to burst through the insulation at its weakest points in spectacular displays of subjective violence. Hall (2014, p. 409) makes the point well when he notes that "controlled deviance overheats and breaks through the control system at its weakest points to appear as plural forms of uncontrolled deviance". The common mistake is to view these breaches, or what Hall (2014) refers to as 'spillage', as erupting against a backdrop of civility and peacefulness, a kind of non-violent zero level (Žižek, 2009). The reality, of course, is that they erupt against a backdrop of intense objective violence inherent in the 'normal', smooth functioning of global capitalism. Think of it this way: if we get an unexpected shock from holding an electric cable (subjective violence), it is only because there is a powerful electric current running through it (objective violence). The electric shock does not materialise from nothing; it comes from the active power source driving the current (stimulated drives and desires).

It is necessary, therefore, to understand that objective violence is hardwired into the capitalist system and manifests in ruthlessly aggressive, but often rule-bound, sociosymbolic competition. As over-stimulated drives and desires crystallise in an ultra-competitive world, we now find ourselves inhabiting a social terrain occupied by a society of enemies (Hall, 2012b). In this socially atomised environment, everyone is considered a threat and every social encounter is potentially risky business as we attempt to successfully navigate our way through permanent social competition. This is demonstrated particularly well in a scene from *Dead Man's Chest* where the crew of the *Black Pearl* attempt to escape from their cages on Isla de Pelegostos. Despite all being part of the same crew, the shipmates battle against each other once they realise that it will only take about six people to crew the ship. As each group struggles to be the first out of the gorge and to the ship, one group of captives continue to climb despite the presence of a guard overhead. This puts the whole crew at risk, and they are eventually spotted and pursued.

In today's atomised society, both personal and business relationships are imbued with increasingly high levels of competition and instrumentalism (Hall & Winlow, 2004). Other over-stimulated energies – latent anxiety, greed, envy – roused by the pseudo-pacification process begin to leak more frequently from eroded socio-cultural restraints, becoming increasingly untethered (Hall, 2012b, 2012c). Within this current climate, the pseudo-pacification process has been stretched beyond its limits and now finds it increasingly difficult to pacify, insulate and redirect the potent energy generated towards socially acceptable activities (Kotzé, 2019). The fundamental upshot is that as stimulation outstrips pacification, the process produces more and more dissociated subjects untethered from any form of collectivism (Kotzé, 2019). Devoid of social obligations and imbued with a firm sense of special liberty, the dissociated subject simply acts "in accordance with the drives and desires oriented toward success in the socio-symbolic competition" (Hall, 2015, p. 134).

It can certainly be suggested that this breakdown in the pseudo-pacification process creates a latently criminogenic climate in which some individuals are willing to inflict harm on others in the process of furthering their own self-interests (Hall, 2012b). For the most part, the *Pirates of the Caribbean* films certainly demonstrate the over-stimulated drives and desires of liberal-capitalism. Throughout the films, we see the intensely stimulated desires and energies that drive consumer capitalism come to the surface, breaking through the ethico-legal restraints which otherwise harness and direct such energies (Raymen, 2018). It is a mistake to think that the majority of crime is non-conformist or proto-political (Hall, 2012c). It is certainly tempting to view the characters of *Pirates of the Caribbean* as swashbuckling heroes, intent on standing against the tyranny of the Company and its vision of progress. However, it is more accurate to conceive their actions as being animated by the same logic that underpins the East India Trading Company. Indeed, the two axioms "trade where necessary and plunder where possible" (Robins, 2012, p. 45), and "take what you can, give nothing back" are remarkably similar. If anything, we should say that Jack Sparrow and his companions *over-identify* with and *hyper-conform* to the potent energies stimulated by the generative core – competitive individualism, aggressive instrumentalism, immediate gratification, the cultivation of envy and the conspicuous display of symbolically charged goods.

As 'criminal undertakers', Sparrow and his companions simply act to 'get things done' in pursuit of their instrumental and/or expressive interests (Hall, 2012a). Their actions are not driven by a desire to escape the system, but precisely to do better *within it*. As the pseudo-pacification process continues to disintegrate, it becomes much harder to pacify with the same intensity as it stimulates, dispersing throughout the social structure subjects who are willing to harm others as they act out their over-stimulated drives and desires (Kotzé, 2019). The theory of the pseudo-pacification process is not proffering some simple deterministic idea of crime causation. Indeed, it is evident that not everyone transcends the ethical and moral norms that keep the generative core in check. Some, with relatively stable sources of social capital, are able to mobilise instrumentalism in suitably pacified ways (Hall & Winlow, 2004). What the pseudo-pacification process identifies is the long-term historical social, cultural and economic context within which crime is made more *likely* to occur. Indeed, as acquisitive-aggressive drives and desires continue to be over-stimulated in a culture of atomised insecurity and competitive individualism (Hall, 2012c), it is perhaps unsurprising to find individuals who will risk extreme harm to others in the pursuit of their own self-interest.

CONCLUSION

The theory of the pseudo-pacification process has emerged as an important corrective to the civilising process originally outlined by Elias (Hall et al., 2008). Throughout the history of the capitalist project, there has never been a move towards civilisation or pacification strictly for their own sake. Instead, only the necessary level of pacification required to lubricate the wheels of the market economy was sought, and for this reason, it is more accurate to refer to the process as *pseudo*-pacification (Hall et al., 2008). Whilst the inner workings of the process can be quite difficult to grasp, the function of the process is fairly straightforward; it works to harness human energy to fuel the expansion of the market economy. The process works to transform economically dysfunctional bouts of subjective violence into aggressively ruthless, yet physically non-violent, forms of objective violence that can be put to work to energise the economic system.

To venture a bit further in our understanding of this complex process, we find the bullet pointed outline provided by Hall and Winlow (2015, p. 116) extremely useful. In particular, the section highlighting the dualistic economic need for pacification is important because it captures the essential shape of the process. Having provided the conditions for the production and circulation of commodities, the process engages in the simultaneous stimulation and pacification of human energy, converting physical aggression into aggressive sociosymbolic competition for wealth and status (Hall & Winlow, 2015). So, what appears at first sight to be the cultivation of civilised tendencies, turns out to be the mobilisation of pseudo-pacified aggressive instrumentalism, stimulated and harnessed to the capitalist market economy (Kotzé, 2019).

Closely associated with the pseudo-pacification process is the concept of special liberty. This is considered to be a general cultural current that operates as a form of subjective permission to inflict harm on others in the pursuit of self-interest (Hall, 2015). In other words, special liberty grants the beholder a sense of entitlement to do whatever it takes to satisfy their desires and interests. Together, pseudo-pacification and special liberty form a powerful, yet highly unstable, macro-cultural current that underlies liberal-capitalism (Hall & Wilson, 2014). Indeed, because the process leans more towards stimulation than pacification, it is prone to breakdown which means that the motivating force produced by the generative core will often break through the regulatory jacket and fuel criminal activity (Hall et al., 2008). This tendency to stimulate and pacify in unequal measure is certainly evident throughout the *Pirates of the Caribbean* films.

Whilst we have used this particular film franchise to explore some of the core facets of the pseudo-pacification process here, other films and TV shows can be equally effective in helping to make sense of this important component of ultra-realism. Having read the chapter, you may be able to identify elements of special liberty and the pseudo-pacification process at play across several popular culture forums. Coupled with a wide range of reading, this is a good way of thinking through some of the theory's more complex components and begin applying what you have learnt to practical examples. Don't just take our word for it; take it from Jack in Study-box 3 (see page 42).

Study-box 3

Student Insight:

Meet Jack, a 20-year-old undergraduate student.

There are a few tips I would give anyone coming to this subject for the first time. Read as much as you can! A reading schedule can be useful, helping to organise and allocate your reading accordingly. Engage with the material and quiz yourself. It is one thing to read something, but to remember and understand a concept is a different conundrum. I found the best way to understand a concept was to test myself. Take your time, this isn't a topic you can breeze over. Once it clicks though, you can begin applying it. I recently applied the pseudo-pacification process to some popular culture, specifically *The Wolf of Wall Street*, for an essay. Through this application I was able to elucidate how Jordan Belfort was hyper-conforming to neoliberalism's overstimulated core of aggressive individualism, self-interest and egoism. In short, he exercised extreme forms of special liberty, prospering as he acted out his overstimulated drives and desires.

Key Takeaway: Don't be intimidated by the complex terminology. Think of ultra-realism like a jigsaw, each core ingredient of ultra-realism plays a significant part in its end theoretical formation.

Study Questions:

- What are the two 'poles' of the pseudo-pacification process, and how do they work to energise the market economy?
- Can you think of some examples where Indiana Jones uses 'special liberty'?
- Why is the pseudo-pacification process prone to breakdown?

Key Reading: Hall, S. (2015) 'What is Criminology About? The Study of Harm, Special Liberty and Pseudo-Pacification in Late-Capitalism's Libidinal Economy'. In Crewe, D. and Lippens, R. (eds) *What is Criminology About? Philosophical Reflections*, pp. 122-140. London: Routledge.

Fig. 3. Study-Box 3.

5

FETISHISTIC DISAVOWAL AND *GAME OF THRONES*

INTRODUCTION

In 2010, factory workers in China made global headlines as one after another threw themselves off the towering dorm buildings that housed assembly-line employees in a desperate protest at working conditions inside. The factory was owned by Foxconn, who manufactured products for Apple, including the iPhone (Merchant, 2018). Cobalt, a rare earth metal central to smartphone production, is mined in extremely hazardous conditions by children as young as six years old in the Democratic Republic of Congo (Kara, 2018). Apple sales, including the iPhone, have doubled since the start of the COVID-19 pandemic (BBC, 2021). We know that natural resources are extracted at great cost to the men, women and children mining rare metals that are then assembled by low-paid workers in extremely poor conditions. Yet we continue to buy those products, regardless of the harms and exploitation at various stages of the extraction and production process. Is it because we do not know or because we are unfeeling and callous? We argue that it is not a question of knowledge but, more likely, that we *know but act as if we don't*. We engage in a psycho-social process of rejecting uncomfortable knowledge so we can continue our lives without guilt or concern.

In this chapter, we explore fetishistic disavowal, the active repression of knowledge into our subconscious, through the world of *Game of Thrones*, the acclaimed HBO series based on the *A Song of Ice and Fire* novels of George R.R. Martin. Along the way, we set out the 'reversal of ideology' (Žižek, 1989), the concept of fetishistic disavowal (Fisher, 2009; Hall & Winlow, 2015) and Kotzé's (2019) degrees of assimilation in conjunction with a discussion of the real existential threat at the heart of *Game of Thrones*: the 'white walkers'. This will primarily involve discussion of two key characters – Jon Snow and Cersei Lannister – but will incorporate other characters too. We will also draw on the *Harry Potter* franchise to illustrate our point. We then explore the utility of this concept in relation to our understanding of existential threats to our society, namely climate change.

UNCOMFORTABLE TRUTHS

Across the eight seasons and, at the time of writing, six novels that comprise the *Game of Thrones* series, much of the focus hinged upon the quest for the 'Iron Throne'. Essentially based in a fantasy version of medieval Europe, George R.R. Martin's fantasy epic follows a number of family houses including the Lannisters, Starks, Targaryens, Baratheons and Tyrells as they vie for control of the seven kingdoms. The series begins with King Robert Baratheon calling upon old friend Eddard (Ned) Stark to join him in the capital of Westeros, King's Landing, as the 'hand of the King' or closest advisor. Baratheon's previous hand has died suddenly, and the suspicion of foul play prompts the king to turn to someone he trusts. Baratheon's subsequent death, through the machinations of his wife, Cersei Lannister, sets in train a series of wars and political intrigues that make up the bulk of the series. However, *Game of Thrones'* very first scene, in season 1, episode 1, shows the viewer, before the first credit sequence or any of the main protagonists appear on screen, where the true threat actually lies.

The first scene features three rangers venturing north 'beyond the wall', a 700-foot-high structure that divides Westeros and protects the civilised world from the 'wildlings'. The rangers of the Night's Watch swear an oath to protect the world of men, and these rangers head into the desolate snowy wasteland to track a wildling party. One spots a thin plume of smoke and, upon closer investigation, stumbles upon a grisly scene: decapitated heads on spikes and mutilated body parts arranged in a symbolic pattern in the snow. The ranger also finds a child's body impaled on a tree, eyes wide open, staring vacantly. He hurries back to his colleagues to show them but upon their return, the bodies have vanished. As they spread out to search, a dark figure rises up behind one ranger, and we see a horrified reaction from another. The scene cuts to the third ranger, alone in the woods. The horses have fled. The solitary ranger turns to see the child we had previously seen impaled on the tree, now standing there, staring at him with ice blue eyes. Both remaining rangers are seen running through the woods. The music implies a chase. They enter a clearing and spot each other, but a figure appears behind one ranger, and we only see the bright blue eyes as the shadowy figure decapitates the ranger and tosses his head on the ground in front of the remaining ranger. The screen fades to black, and the first credit sequence commences.

This is the first scene of the entire series. The audience is told, before any of the main characters are introduced, that something exists beyond the wall, something terrifying, something that brings the dead to life. Later in the episode, the sole surviving ranger is found fleeing south and brought by cavalry officers to Winterfell, the key city in the north. Ned Stark is the Warden of the North and oath-bound to protect the North and, by extension, the island of Westeros, from threats beyond the wall. An honourable man, Stark upholds the laws, including sentencing to death any deserter from the Night's Watch. Our terrified ranger is brought before Stark and, although accepting of his fate as a deserter, warns Stark of the threat. Stark doesn't respond but carries out the execution as "he who passes sentence should swing the sword". His ten-year-old son, Bran Stark is present and while the scene is ostensibly about a lesson in duty and honour for young Bran, it is instructive for us:

> *Bran: "Is it true he saw the white walkers?"*
> *Ned: "The white walkers have been gone for thousands of years".*
> *Bran: "So he was lying?"*
> *Ned: "A mad man sees what he sees".*

The white walkers have long since disappeared from Westeros, so why should Stark believe him? Very quickly, the story changes direction and becomes focused on palace intrigue in the court of King Robert Baratheon. The ranger's encounter with a white walker represents an encounter with the Real (Hall, 2012a). What Stark dismisses as 'madness' is instead the consequences of a traumatic encounter with something out of place, something horrifying. The ranger has encountered the obscene Real at the heart of Westeros and in that sense does not disavow the knowledge he has gained. At this point, for the other characters in *Game of Thrones*, alternative explanations carry enough weight to reject or disbelieve what they are being told. They have invested too much in the fantasy-construction that shapes their Symbolic Order to believe differently. We can briefly turn to the *Harry Potter* franchise for another example. Voldemort, he who should not be named, is believed vanquished although his return is the catalyst for the action across the seven books and films. In *The Order of the Phoenix,* Harry Potter is on trial for using magic in front of a muggle. At his defence, Professor Dumbledore presents clear evidence that Harry's use of magic was to protect against Dementors, who were controlled by Voldemort. Rather than accept the evidence, the Minister for Magic, Cornelius Fudge, dramatically announces "he's not back!". Rather than accept the evidence in front of him, he suspends belief in order to disavow unsettling knowledge. In the 14 years since Voldemort vanished, Fudge has acquired power and status, and it rests on the belief that Voldemort is dead. His comfortable world is at risk of disruption and rather than accept reality, he chooses disavowal. The remainder of the chapter considers how this process works.

RETHINKING IDEOLOGY

To begin, how does ideology work? Here we ask the reader to move beyond the Marxist interpretation of ideology as 'false consciousness'. Marx and Engels suggested that ideology acted as a mask that mediated our relationship to reality, blocking our access to the real world by throwing a veil across our eyes and preventing recognition of the fundamental iniquities of capitalist society (Marx, 1990; Marx & Engels, 1998). In this configuration, and in Marx's understanding of historical materialism as the motor of progress, political revolution and the destruction of capitalism could only come from the recognition of this false consciousness. The working class, as the agents of historical change, needed to collectively lift the veil and recognise the true nature of its exploitation. This indicates that ideology works at the level of thought; that in our daily lives, material realities show us the nature of exploitation but we *think* that things will get better, that things aren't as bad as they seem. When we wise up to that exploitation, we will seek alternative configurations that offer liberation.

However, Žižek (1989) perceptively suggests that the postmodern turn decimated the notion of universality, truth and grand narrative:

> *Ideology is not a dreamlike illusion that we build to escape insupportable reality; in its basic dimension it is a fantasy-construction which serves as a support for our 'reality' itself: an 'illusion' which structures our effective, real social relations and thereby masks some insupportable, real, impossible kernel.*
>
> *(Žižek, 1989, p. 45)*

The subject of our late modern society is too knowing to be duped by universal truths, media and state propaganda, or grand narratives that attempt to explain the world in unifying terms (Lloyd, 2017). A cynical distance has opened between knowledge and action; we recognise the particular interests behind the ideology and see the distance between the ideological mask and reality but still find reasons to retain the mask. We know that capitalist society is exploitative (Pemberton, 2016). We know that left to its own devices, the natural tendency of capitalist society will create greater and more divisive forms of inequality (Piketty, 2014). We know that consumer culture is both ecologically unsustainable and subjectively dissatisfying (Hall, Winlow, & Ancrum, 2008; Raymen & Smith, 2019). However, despite knowing these things, *we act as if we do not*. In this sense, ideology works at the level of action and not thought (Žižek, 1989).

So, if this is the case, how does it work? This is where the concept of fetishistic disavowal appears. The subject willingly represses inconvenient knowledge into its unconscious to continue to act in the world (Hall, 2012a). We disavow troubling or problematic knowledge so we can continue to live our lives as we see fit, to focus on the things that are important to us. Returning to our earlier example, we know that cobalt and other precious minerals are mined by child slaves in the Democratic Republic of Congo and that those minerals are used to make the smartphone screens that play such a fundamental part of our lives (Kara, 2018). As Kuldova (2019, p. 769) notes, "the fact that the activists fail time and again at changing the actual behaviour of consumers whom they repeatedly enlighten should already tell us that ignorance is not the actual problem here". Rather than face the uncomfortable truth and change our consumer habits, we repress that knowledge; we *fetishistically disavow* our knowledge of this inconvenient truth and carry on as normal (Fisher, 2009). On a more basic level, we have all been in conversations where people will change the subject rather than face some political controversy; we *choose* what to repress into our unconscious while simultaneously *act out* every day to reproduce existing structures and cultures (Hall & Winlow, 2015).

We frequently disavow the obscene Real at the heart of our capitalist system. On some level, most people are aware that the democratic structures in which we place our faith have been corrupted; narrowed like hardened arteries following years of neglect and abuse to the point where candidates for office, from all political persuasions, represent a narrow set of interests (Winlow, Hall, Treadwell, & Briggs, 2015). We know that government favours big business, financial interests and the elites and that markets come before people (Harvey, 2010; Streeck, 2016). Yet at each election, we act as if we don't know these things. Yes, we are often happy to admit that we know voting makes little difference, that parties do not care about people like us, but we still arrive at the ballot box and choose between the lesser of two evils. At the level of knowledge, we are aware of this, yet we repress this knowledge and act as if we do not know in order to maintain the symbolic fiction that allows us to carry on with our lives. We know the system is designed to favour a narrow band of oligarchs who will continue to profit handsomely while far more people slip into poverty and precarious existence, yet we continue to act as if we do not. The knowledge is too unsettling and so, for many of us, we repress it in order to function normally. In *Game of Thrones,* the obscene Real is the threat of the white walkers and the army of reanimated corpses that do their bidding. We know this from the outset and while the characters are not initially aware of the threat, over the course of the series, they do become increasingly cognisant of this growing danger. By the later series, the white walkers present a clear and present threat that is almost impossible to ignore. However, a process of disavowal repeatedly occurs as many continue to act as if they do not know this. They maintain their focus on the Iron Throne and dominance over the seven kingdoms. Their internecine squabbles are prioritised over the obscene Real that threatens their existence.

DEGREES OF ASSIMILATION: DREAMING COMFORTABLY WHILE WESTEROS FREEZES...

While the concept of fetishistic disavowal offers us significant insight into the complex relationship between unconscious, obscene Real and Symbolic Order, we have to push further. In *Game of Thrones*, Jon Snow consistently identifies the white walkers and their leader, the Night King, as the existential threat at the heart of their world. His insistence on preparing to fight this army forces him into new alliances with former enemies thus upsetting traditional political and tribal allegiances. By season five, this costs him his life, murdered at the hands of his own disgruntled men. Fortunately, this is a fantasy drama and Snow is brought back to life by Melisandre, a priestess of the Lord of Light. Upon his resurrection, Snow resumes his original plan to prevent the white walkers' intended genocide. From his first encounters with the dead and the white walkers, Snow never wavers from his belief that they pose a threat greater than any family or house vying for the Iron Throne, often at great personal cost. In no way can we suggest that Snow disavows his knowledge of the white walkers to go about his normal life. So, where does this leave the concept of fetishistic disavowal?

A fruitful extension of the concept of disavowal emerges from ultra-realist criminology: Kotzé's (2019) 'dream myth' and degrees of assimilation. Rather than accepting disavowal as something that happens to each subject in the same way and to the same degree, this concept recognises that we assimilate into the dream myth of a dominant Symbolic Order differently. Each subject is assimilated by degrees, according to their proximity to the obscene Real. There are those fully assimilated, partially assimilated and unassimilated. The 'dream myth' in our society is one of modernity as a liberalising force towards unalloyed progress (Hall, 2012a). Yes, there are stumbles along the way, but the organising ideological narrative has been one of progressive improvement in standards of living, healthcare and education, alongside a civilising tendency that aligns with a historic decline in crime (Elias, 2000; Pinker, 2012). In *Game of Thrones*, the dream myth is that white walkers and other magical beings have been consigned to history and that true power lies in the political and military might of whoever occupies the Iron Throne. The expenditure of libidinal energy throughout much of the story arc is geared towards the acquisition and maintenance of domination and power, manifested in the Iron Throne and the occupation of King's Landing. The forging and breaking of alliances, political intrigue and military campaigns are all geared towards this end. However, not all are fully assimilated within this dream myth.

Jon Snow's proximity to the obscene Real is clear: he has fought white walkers beyond the wall and, at the Battle of Hardhome, watches the Night King reanimate Snow's own dead soldiers to fight against him. Seeing the dead rise and take up arms against him represents a traumatic encounter with the obscene Real that prevents Snow from assimilating into the dream myth that white walkers are an old fairy tale, a relic of bygone ages, that the real struggle is for control of the Iron Throne. Jon Snow therefore represents the 'unassimilated' (Kotzé, 2019). Unlike Cornelius Fudge in *The Order of the Phoenix*, there are no alternative explanations that allow him to disavow what he has seen. Snow's prolonged over-proximity to the obscene Real results in the complete disintegration of the symbolic reality or fantasy-construction at the heart of Westerosi culture. He has no access to the comforting 'sense of reality' that the dream myth affords; he has seen and knows too much to be enthralled by the dream myth. He cannot disavow knowledge in the same way that those living on crime-ridden housing estates cannot disavow that knowledge to accept the fantasy that crime is in decline due to a civilising tendency at the heart of our culture.

Cersei Lannister, on the other hand, represents the 'fully assimilated' (Kotzé, 2019). From the beginning of the show, Cersei is preoccupied with power and the supremacy of her family dynasty. As the wife of King Robert Baratheon, Cersei has accepted his infidelities and boorish ways whilst secretly siring three children with her brother Jaime. After engineering her husband's death, Cersei concentrates political and military force first behind her eldest son, the psychopathic Joffrey and, second, her youngest son Tommen. After their deaths, she seizes power herself. Geographically, King's Landing is remote from the north and the events percolating beyond the wall. As a medieval state, there is no internet or 24-hour news to relay events from far-flung places so her knowledge of the white walkers, Jon Snow and the brewing conflict in the North comes from message-bearing ravens and travellers returning to the capital. These events are peripheral to her own troubles: the Battle of the Five Armies, the deaths of her children and father, her feud with the Tyrells and Martells, her subjugation at the hands of the Faith Militant and her final concentration and solidification of power.

Cersei's proximity to these events and the threat of the white walkers is so distant that it becomes easy to ignore this threat. She disavows this knowledge repeatedly and concentrates on what she believes to be more pressing challenges. By season seven, the threat from the North has manifested in King's Landing with Jon Snow, Daenerys Targaryen and Tyrion Lannister arriving with evidence of the Night King's power and threat. They call an armistice with a view to joining forces in the face of the obscene Real and at the meeting reveal a reanimated corpse that lunges at Cersei. Her proximity to the obscene Real changes significantly but, crucially, only momentarily; Cersei is 'fully assimilated' in the Westerosi dream myth and willingly interprets the external reality in a distorted or incomplete way. So, while ostensibly agreeing to a truce to fight the Night King, she instead uses the opportunity to gain advantage by double-crossing everyone. Cersei demonstrates how the 'fully assimilated' are prone to self-deceit; in choosing to be deceived, she allows herself to become a 'willing dupe' precisely so that she can maintain her *sense of reality* (Kotzé, 2019). Seemingly unhindered by the presentation of countervailing evidence – the reanimated corpse – Cersei is able to maintain a significant distance from the obscene Real and fundamentally disavows the knowledge that she acquires at the dragon pit summit. She acts as if she does not know that the Night King is raising an army of the dead intent on destroying all in its path. She conveniently represses this knowledge to continue acting as if consolidation of her position on the Iron Throne is what *really* matters. Cersei also affords us the chance to follow Kuldova's (2019) distinction between *disavowal* (I know quite well how things are, but still…)

and *fetishistic disavowal* (I don't only know how things are, but also how they appear to me, and nonetheless…). Disavowal is the cynical gap between knowledge and action, whereas fetishistic disavowal involves the pleasure that accompanies awareness of the gap between knowledge and reality. The fetishist knows that the object is both material and symbolic/sacred and still derives pleasure from it. In the same way that we derive pleasure from consumer purchases that require our repression of uncomfortable truths, Cersei fetishises power and the Iron Throne and derives pleasure and satisfaction from vanquishing her enemies, defeating the odds and gaining control. In order to do this, she disavows the unsettling truth about the white walkers and represents full assimilation in the dream myth that has provided the Symbolic Order that shapes her entire existence.

If we switch from the fantasy world of *Game of Thrones* to our world, we can see examples of fetishistic disavowal. In a political-economic context, the West has largely outsourced production and resource extraction to the global South and East, particularly China. In the West, we have acknowledged the threat of climate change and have begun to challenge fossil fuel use and excessive carbon emissions. However, as Pitron (2020, p. 177) astutely observes,

> *Relocating our dirty industries has helped keep Western consumers in the dark about the true environmental cost of our lifestyles, while giving other nation-states free rein to extract and process minerals in even worse conditions than would have applied had they still been mined in the West, without the slightest regard for the environment. The effects of returning mining operations to the West would be positive. We would instantly realise – to our horror – the true cost of our self-declared modern, connected, and green world.*

We have moved production from our immediate line of sight thus allowing us to disavow knowledge of its harmful and destructive nature. What we do not see cannot hurt us and the troubling knowledge that does emerge through news reports and Netflix documentaries can be disavowed and suppressed into our unconscious. We are not faced with the obscene Real of the environmental damage caused by both resource extraction *and enjoyment of our consumer lifestyles*. Western consumers can continue 'dreaming comfortably' in the belief that digital technology and clean energy will tackle climate change and that a fundamental reconsideration of our social, political, economic and cultural landscape can be avoided. We know that our conception of freedom is an ideological and symbolic fiction and that underpinning that freedom are a range of exploitative relations, but we continue to follow our idea of freedom and disavow the troubling knowledge that brings the obscene Real into view. We *know* climate change is likely and its impact could be devastating, but we continue to act as if we do not know.

CONCLUSION

Our society is one characterised by inequality, harm, exploitation and aggressive and ruthless competition that damages people, communities and the environment. Our problem is not one of knowledge or a lack thereof. We know this. There is no fundamental misrecognition of social reality. Ideology acts as a fantasy-construction that creates a sociosymbolic fiction that structures a *sense of reality* and prevents a traumatic encounter with the obscene Real. We cynically distance ourselves from troubling knowledge in order to maintain the sense of freedom and enjoyment afforded by liberal capitalism. This process of fetishistic disavowal demonstrates the relationship between subject and ideology, the active role played by repression and our unconscious, and the distance between knowledge and action. It also demonstrates the value of agency and is not a mechanistic determination on the part of political economic ideology; each subject represses uncomfortable truths according to their own position within the sociosymbolic order and based on the level of assimilation within the structuring dream myth.

The challenges we face as a society are visible for all to see. It is no secret that climate change and environmental harm represent an existential crisis. Mass migration, driven by geopolitical conflict, resource depletion and climate change are both inevitable and already taking place (Briggs, 2020; Parenti, 2011). Technological advancement, zoonotic disease, violence and social disorder, structural labour market upheaval and many other issues also zoom into view when we look closely. However, much of this is unsettling knowledge, and we individually and collectively engage in acts of disavowal to prevent these truths imposing upon the sociosymbolic order that structures our lives, provides a sense of reality and represents the contours of pleasure and freedom. What *Game of Thrones* shows us is the tendency to repress knowledge that questions our sense of reality. The white walkers, and Voldemort in the *Harry Potter* films, represent an encounter with the obscene Real that lies outside the structuring fantasy in which most characters have invested. Jon Snow shows us that degrees of assimilation are apparent within that relationship between subject and ideology; his over-proximity and exposure to the obscene Real of the Night King, the white walkers and the army of the dead preclude assimilation and foreclose disavowal. For others, such as Cersei Lannister, their complete assimilation reflects their libidinal investment in the Symbolic Order and the gap between knowledge and action. In the next chapter, we consider ways to overcome this process of disavowal in order to face the trauma of the Real. As Ciaran notes in Study-box 4 (see page 54), there are many things we encounter in our everyday lives that we choose to disavow, but there is value in reflecting on what we choose to ignore, and why.

Study-box 4

Student Insight:

Meet Ciaran, a 25-year-old postgraduate student.

To put it simply, fetishistic disavowal is when you know that something is happening, but you actively choose to ignore it. A relatable way in which we may do this on a daily basis is, for example, seeing that your bedroom is a mess, but choosing to simply ignore the mess as if it does not exist all around you. Obviously, this is not the intended way of viewing this theory, however, take that mess in your room no matter how big or small it may be, and apply it to the social realm. The "mess" becomes homelessness, subjective and objective violence, class divide, job losses, all the things we encounter in our daily lives that we simply choose to ignore, yet we are acutely aware that they exist around us. Ultimately, this form of disavowal prevails throughout many aspects of life, and it is worth reflecting upon what we choose to ignore as individuals and as a wider collective.

Key Takeaway: Consider the classic movie *They Live*, put on your sunglasses and see what you have been ignoring all around you.

Study Questions:

- What is the 'reversal of ideology' and how does it relate to fetishistic disavowal?
- How do Kotzé's 'degrees of assimilation' work?
- Can you think of other characters in *Game of Thrones* who represent the unassimilated, partially assimilated and fully assimilated?

Key Reading: Kotzé, J. (2019) *The Myth of the 'Crime Decline': Exploring Change and Continuity in Crime and Harm.* London: Routledge. Chapter 6.

Fig. 4. Study-Box 4.

6

ENLIGHTENED CATASTROPHISM AND *INFERNO*

INTRODUCTION

In the epilogue to Dan Brown's (2014) *Inferno*, we find Professor Robert Langdon engrossed in Dante's classic work, *The Divine Comedy*. Reflecting on the salience of Dante's words, Langdon begins to recognise with greater perceptibility the implications of inaction in dangerous times, acknowledging that "when it came to the circumstances of the world, denial had become a global pandemic" (Brown, 2014, p. 619). Indeed, we saw in the previous chapter that engaging in persistent bouts of fetishistic disavowal has become an almost endemic feature of our contemporary society. We frequently engage in activities we know are likely to sustain or even intensify global inequalities, environmental degradation and ecocide, but continue to act *as if we do not know*. Instead of facing our troubles head on, we choose to forget these unsettling realities and force them out of consciousness so that we may continue unhindered in our daily routines (Winlow, 2019). However, Winlow (2013, p. 32) makes it very clear that "we cannot go on as we are". In fact, Dupuy (2015) notes that we are currently living in the shadow cast by impending catastrophes that threaten to wipe out the human race. Surely, then, the fundamental question is, 'what can we do to prevent this from happening?' By drawing on the concept of enlightened catastrophism, this chapter will attempt to sketch out an ultra-realist response to this question. In doing so, we draw upon the book and film adaptation of *Inferno*, as well as the 2008 version of *The Day the Earth Stood Still*.

LIVING IN THE SHADOW OF CATASTROPHE

Neoliberalism has arguably become "the defining political economic paradigm of our time" (McChesney, 1999, p. 7). Put simply, neoliberalism can be described as the latest phase of capitalism but one which is more ruthless, predatory and selfish (James, 2008). Since the 1980s, neoliberalism has framed the way we organise our lives and influenced our relationships with others, encouraging us to put profit before people (Whitehead, 2018). It has worked to reconfigure moral boundaries, weaken social ties and eroded any sort of ethical obligation to each other. In the place of hopes for collective solidarity, a new anthropological logic has emerged that both produces and reproduces demonised and regulated 'others' (Whitehead, 2018). Within this context, and over the past four decades, neoliberal consumer capitalism has helped cultivate harmful subjectivities characterised by greed, envy, narcissism, competitive individualism and self-interest (Raymen, 2016). As previously demonstrated, the active solicitation of the subject into the prevailing norms, values and dispositions of neoliberal consumer capitalism means that the motivation to act is likely to manifest in particular ways (Lloyd, 2018b). We are, in other words, more likely to reject social solidarity in favour of competitive individualism, which means we are more likely to risk harm to others to further our own interests and satisfy our desires (Raymen, 2016). The latent criminogenesis of this cultural current has already been demonstrated.

There is certainly a complex interrelationship between the configuration of our current sociosymbolic order and subjective motivation. By exploring this we can begin to understand that some manifestations of crime and harm are symptoms of capitalism's zemiological environment (Kotzé, 2021). Life itself has been deeply affected by this negative capitalism (Taylor, 2013). In addition to injecting violence and aggressive competition into every aspect of our lives, neoliberal consumer capitalism has increased the cost of living as well as the levels of unemployment, homelessness and poverty. In a word, *negativity* characterises contemporary neoliberal capitalism (Taylor, 2013). Smaligo (2014) points out that depression and anxiety are natural responses to this situation. Couched in terms of chemical imbalances, we are encouraged to view these issues as *personal* failings to be remedied by mass-market pharmaceuticals, instead of emanating from a severely deapted sociosymbolic order. It might be fair to say, then, that capitalism lies at the heart of the most pressing social problems we face today (Winlow, 2019).

It's not just people who are affected by neoliberal consumer capitalism. Indeed, Smaligo (2014, p. 124) argues that "capitalism is destroying the ecological basis of life on the planet". He is certainly not alone in thinking this.

Fuggle (2018) highlights that whilst the term 'late' capitalism gives us the impression that it is nearing the end, what is actually coming to an end is the sustainability of human existence. Whitehead (2015, p. 29, original emphasis) also notes that "neoliberal capitalism constitutes a politico-economic *and* ethical system concerned with the *end* of human existence". The evidence is all around us. Chemical contamination of soil and water, deforestation (Smaligo, 2014), widespread climate change, loss of biodiversity (Fuggle, 2018), global pollution, acidification of oceans, climatic refugees (Neyrat, 2019), depletion of fossil resources, new strains of infectious disease (Dupuy, 2015), the list goes on. It is not that we are unaware of these threats. Indeed, the dramatic consequences of global warming were made known to us more than a quarter-century ago (Dupuy, 2015). Similarly, whilst commenting on the COVID-19 pandemic, Žižek (2020) notes that we were told time and again that a much stronger epidemic than SARS and Ebola was waiting just around the corner.

Whilst we are convinced of the truth of these predictions, we do not take them seriously (Žižek, 2020). Even when we have all the information to conclude that catastrophe is imminent, we do not believe it; we do not believe what we know to be true (Dupuy, 2009, 2014). We stand on the brink of destruction interpassively hoping that someone, somewhere, will act on our behalf to avert disaster (Winlow, 2017); believing that science and technology will come to our rescue (Dupuy, 2013). The naivety of this is called out brilliantly by Klaatu in *The Day the Earth Stood Still*: "Your problem is not technology; the problem is you. You lack the will to change...you treat the world as you treat each other". Despite the irrefutable knowledge that we are fast approaching the Sixth Extinction (Neyrat, 2019), we remain resolute in *not* taking radical action precisely because "we cannot bring ourselves to face up to the implications of what we know" (Dupuy, 2015, p. 10). In conversation with Klaatu, Mr Wu identifies the tragedy of our commitment to fetishistic disavowal: "The tragedy is, they know what's going to happen to them. They sense it. But they can't seem to do anything about it".

Klaatu makes it clear that our salvation will come at great cost to our way of life. We must make radical changes, although it is not always easy for us to agree on what to change. This is because we are embroiled in a culture of emotivism, which means that moral and evaluative judgements simply reflect pluralistic expressions of self-interest and preferences (Raymen, 2019a). Accordingly, drives to stimulate real change are often framed in ways that denote a need for us to act *against* our self-interest and desires (Raymen, 2019a). Against a backdrop framed by a cultural injunction to enjoy *now* (Myers, 2003), such drives are often met with staunch resistance. Take the issue of human overpopulation, for example. The fact of the matter is that human overpopulation continues to be a pressing issue that risks the very viability of our environment (Davis, Arnocky, & Stroink, 2019). Bognar (2019, p. 320) points out that overpopulation is perhaps the most important factor driving climate change and that "it is rarely acknowledged that the worst thing you can do to the climate is to have children". Indeed, evidence suggests that compared to other proenvironmental behaviours such as recycling, consuming a plant-based diet and buying energy efficient products, having fewer children has a larger positive impact on the environment (Davis et al., 2019). Yet, for many years, the idea of limiting population growth had been considered taboo (Bognar, 2019). This is captured particularly well by Bertrand Zobrist in the film *Inferno*. During his public address he decries the fact that despite overpopulation contributing to every single global ill, serious birth control measures don't stand a chance:

> *'Outrages! Violation of my rights, invasion of my privacy, don't tell me what to do'. And still, we keep attacking our own environment. There have been 5 major extinctions in the earth's history, unless we take bold, immediate action, the 6th extinction will be our own.*

It seems that whilst bold action is off limits, minor concessions can be made so long as they do not impinge too heavily upon one's sovereign desires. Minor inconveniences are barely tolerable; make sure we recycle, drive electric cars, use paper straws and so on. However, in the typical style of neoliberal consumer capitalism, this does not compel us to reduce our consumption. On the contrary, we are encouraged to consume *more*. As Fisher (2009, p. 15) points out, "all we have to do is buy the right products". An IKEA advert recently captured this alluring logic. The opening scene depicts a 'garbage asteroid' hurtling towards earth. As the camera pans out, we can see that it is made up of all our consumer waste: toys, electronics, plastic, fast-food containers, etc. The news suddenly appears and a reporter notes that "Some climate experts say time is running out to prevent disaster unless we seriously change our habits". The rest of the advert is filled with up-beat scenes of people making small adjustments here and there and as they do, the asteroid begins to break apart. The underlying message is clear: *no serious change is needed* to prevent catastrophe; small tweaks here and there will be sufficient to avert disaster. The reality, of course, is that we know fine well that this is not enough. It is, as Zobrist notes, "like swinging a flyswatter at an incoming asteroid. The time bomb is no longer ticking. It has already gone off" (Brown, 2014, p. 147).

Let us be clear, 'green consumption' – designed to assuage the consumer of their guilt – will not save us. In fact, in many ways, it is actually counter-productive as it serves to provide only the appearance of change which prevents real change from taking place (See Kotzé, 2020). As the shadow of catastrophe grows ever darker, capitalism remains stubbornly resistant to radical change, and we continue to rely on market solutions to resolve intractable problems (Briggs, Ellis, Lloyd, & Telford, 2020). Paradoxically, the more we persuade ourselves of the efficacy of these solutions, the faster we rush headlong into the abyss (Dupuy, 2015). There is a simple reason for this. The recognition of risk is diminished in proportion to the extent to which we think solutions exist (Dupuy, 2009). In order to prevent catastrophe we need to believe that it will occur *before* it happens. However, it appears that catastrophe is only made credible *once it has occurred*; it "becomes possible only by 'possibilising' itself" (Dupuy, 2009, p. 9). This leaves us in a tricky situation, how do we prevent a catastrophe that has not yet been made credible? The answer is both simple and difficult at the same time. We must believe what we know to be true and make catastrophe credible by seeing its very real existence as part of our future (Dupuy, 2015). In short, we need an antidote to fetishistic disavowal.

ULTRA-REALISM AND ENLIGHTENED CATASTROPHISM

The antidote to fetishistic disavowal, we would argue, is enlightened catastrophism. Originally devised by Dupuy (2009), ultra-realists stress the need to adopt this philosophical attitude and ditch unworldly optimism (see Kotzé, 2020; Winlow, 2017). In contrast to ideas surrounding the concepts of risk and precaution, enlightened catastrophism encourages us to think of catastrophe as an unavoidable event that has *already happened* (Claisse & Delvenne, 2015). Far from representing some kind of fatalism, enlightened catastrophism is a form of optimism grounded in reason (Dupuy, 2014). The method entails participating in an act of mental projection to take an imaginative leap into the future, placing ourselves in the moment following the catastrophic event. From there, we can look back to our present and see catastrophe as our *fate*; but a fate we may yet choose to avoid (Dupuy, 2013). By engaging in this temporal loop between future and present, we are able to see catastrophe 'possibilise' itself and thus achieve the credibility required for us to mobilise all our resources to prevent it from happening.

The ability to believe what we already know to be true materialises only at the moment we recognise disaster as a foregone conclusion, and it is only at this point will we do what is necessary to try and prevent it (Fuggle, 2018). This resonates with what Žižek (2017) refers to as a zero point of hopelessness. The way out resides in our acceptance of the total hopelessness of our situation because "it is only when we despair and don't know anymore what to do that change can be enacted" (Žižek, 2017, p. x). This is depicted nicely in *The Day the Earth Stood Still.* In the scene, Professor Barnhardt is clarifying with Klaatu that it was only after his world was threatened with destruction did they evolve, before acknowledging that this is precisely where we are now: "You say we're on the brink of destruction and you're right. But its only on the brink that people find the will to change, only at the precipice do we evolve". This is further illustrated towards the end of the film where Dr Hellen Benson catches a glimpse of the organic eating cloud of micro-bots. In this moment, catastrophe – the end of the human race – is at once made both credible and possible; the future is both real and *already here.* This represents humanity's zero point of hopelessness that spurs our intent to change as Hellen entreats Klaatu to stop the 'process'. Whilst most films are poor vehicles for enlightened catastrophism – with endings that usually, and somewhat arrogantly, position ourselves and our science and technology as the saviours of the day – we suggest that *The Day the Earth Stood Still* is a reasonable exercise in enlightened catastrophism. This is because it provides us with a glimpse of our *fate*, the devastation wrought as the Earth is re-set, before returning us back to the present from our mental projection into the future as the 'process' is halted. At this point we 'begin by coming back' (Neyrat, 2019), ready to do what must be done in order to survive.

Through the process of enlightened catastrophism, we can approach a zero point of hopelessness. However, instead of letting this depressive glimpse into the future paralyse us, we must have the courage to be afraid and turn "our hopelessness into the necessity of radical politics" (Neyrat, 2019, p. 90). A politics, Fuggle (2018) argues, of time. That is to say, a politics which looks beyond our incessant obsession with the present. This is an important point because, despite the outward appearance that capitalism is holding itself to account by promoting – or more accurately, commodifying – green consumption, ethical responsibility and action has been deferred to a future that will never come (Fuggle, 2018). The tenets of neoliberal consumer capitalism enjoin us to enjoy *now!* Forget deferred gratification, don't worry about the harms you may be inflicting on others and the environment, or the debt you might accrue whilst doing it, just enjoy every minute of every day. In this context, it is difficult to focus on the future and the impending catastrophes because the future, and even the present, are forced to give way to a privileging of the *instant* (Fuggle, 2018). The pressure to ensure that we do not postpone commodified gratification is intense, so much so that one feels guilty for *not* indulging one's desires (Ellis et al., 2018). As Ellis et al. (2018, p. 25) go one to note "the absence of pleasure weighs heavy upon the psyche".

There can be little doubt that capitalism has captured most of us at the deep psychological level of drive and desire (Hall, 2015). Nothing illustrates this better than some of our responses to the COVID-19 lockdown measures. Briggs et al. (2020) highlight how far from stimulating a coherent vision of an alternative future, lockdown reinforced and even intensified our commitment to the existing Symbolic Order. Even in the midst of a global pandemic, visualisations of the self in a 'post-coronavirus' future bore the same features as pre-lockdown social life (Briggs et al., 2020). Our commitment to McDonalds, Nando's, cosmetics and fashion remained unyielding. When all was said and done, aspirations for a reconfigured future were "undone by the strength of subjective desire for existing consumer lifestyles" (Briggs et al., 2020, p. 842). Why did this pandemic that cost the lives of so many not constitute an 'event' that could provide the catalyst for change? The answer is simple. It was never made credible. Even after 'possibilising' itself we never truly believed what we knew to be true. We continued to think that the worst – whatever that looked like – could still be avoided and therefore did not really believe that it threatened us (Dupuy, 2013), at least not enough to make sustained radical change.

It is not a lack of knowledge that is our problem, it is that knowledge is not transformed into belief capable of stimulating meaningful action (Dupuy, 2014). To say that we bury our heads in the sand is perhaps an oversimplification. Is there not a panoply of initiatives and projects tasked with trying to avert all kinds of impending calamities? At this very moment is there not a range of activist movements winning small battles all over the social landscape? Does this not demonstrate that knowledge is transformed into action? Unfortunately, the answer to this last question is 'no'. Think of it this way; if knowledge and action exist as two poles on a continuum, then belief would sit right in the middle. In the absence of belief, knowledge is not transformed into action but into *pseudo-activity* that provides the appearance of change precisely so that nothing has to change (Kotzé, 2020). Commodified gestures and piecemeal adjustments here and there do not stimulate change. Instead, by evoking the possibility of change they enthusiastically shove the zero point of hopelessness further back into the corner of our minds, ensuring that appropriate solutions will *not* be acted upon (Žižek, 2017). Zobrist makes the point well, if a little bluntly, in *Inferno:*

> *Open your eyes! We are on the brink of the end of humanity, and our world leaders are sitting in boardrooms commissioning studies on solar power, recycling, and hybrid automobiles?... Ozone depletion, lack of water, and pollution are not the disease – they are the symptoms... Unless we face world population head-on, we are doing nothing more than sticking a Band-Aid on a fast-growing cancerous tumour.*
>
> *(Brown, 2014, p. 192)*

The first step towards averting catastrophe is to make it credible, not as a future threat but as our *fate* if we carry on as we are. Towards this end we must move beyond the baseless optimism of liberal social science because, as Winlow (2017, p. 182) notes, it "actively prevents us from taking the steps that must be taken if we are to do what needs to be done". Let us be clear here. We are not advocating Zobrist's idea for mass sterilisation. What we are advocating here is a need to participate in a gesture of refusal to engage in counterproductive pseudo-activity (Kotzé, 2020). It is only by *not* indulging in fabricated forms of optimism and the promise of a better future that we can begin to muster the courage to be afraid; to see catastrophe as our fate. By utilising enlightened catastrophism as a vehicle to confront a zero point of hopelessness, we can begin to mobilise all our energy and resources and put these to work to prevent catastrophe. Admirable as they may appear, bouts of pseudo-activity in the form of charity, micro-resistance and simulated transgressions do not stimulate the kind of radical change required to avert disaster. On the contrary, they prevent real change. They serve as a buffer against the shock of recognition and conscious acceptance of the hopelessness of our situation; a recognition that should compel us to begin to do what needs to be done to "arrest our slow descent into the chaos of the future" (Winlow, 2017, p. 191).

Ultra-realism is often characterised as bleak, overly pessimistic and depressing. Yet, seeing such characteristics as inherent in the theory itself as opposed to the world we live in is like chastising the mirror for the way we look in the morning. Indeed, is it not bleak and depressing that humanity does its utmost to imperil its own survival (Dupuy, 2015)? In the epigraph to *Revitalizing Criminological Theory*, Hall and Winlow (2015) remind us of Thomas Hardy's sage words: "If a way to the better there be, it lies in taking a full look at the worst". Ultra-realism takes this to heart and demonstrates a commitment to "explaining the world as it is, warts and all" (Winlow & Hall, 2013, p. 175). Remember that adopting a pedagogy of enlightened catastrophism is not fatalism, but a form of optimism founded on reason (Dupuy, 2014). We can avoid catastrophe if we are able to make it credible before it occurs, if we 'possibilise' it through the metaphysics of projected time and accept it as our fate *if* we do not commit to radical change (Dupuy, 2009). This requires us to dispense with undue optimism and utilise all the available evidence to construct an accurate picture of the future and then act in accordance with that representation (Claisse & Delvenne, 2015).

CONCLUSION

Committed to confronting "neoliberal capitalism's worldwide zemiological environment full in the face" (Hall & Winlow, 2018a, p. 54), ultra-realism digs beneath the surface of abstracted empiricism and relativist emotivism to reveal the lived experiences of everyday life. Depressing as these may be, ultra-realism encourages us to face up to the realities of our time and take the necessary steps to set us on a different path. At this point it is worth reminding ourselves that many of the global threats we face today are often framed as being the result of ignorance, of a lack of knowledge. If only we knew about the impacts of global warming, human overpopulation, austerity, labour saving technologies and mass unemployment, inequality, modern slavery, etc. we would be able to do something about it. Yet, the problem is not that we do not know about these issues and their consequences. The problem is that we continue to act *as if* we do not know, demonstrating an extreme unwillingness to believe what we know to be true (Dupuy, 2015).

As a potential antidote to this fetishistic disavowal, ultra-realists suggest that we adopt the philosophical attitude of enlightened catastrophism. This unique framework offers us the opportunity to step outside of ourselves and see our predicament as it really is (Dupuy, 2015). By participating in an act of mental projection we can take an imaginative leap into the future and place ourselves in the moment following catastrophe. Identifying the causal chain, we can see this future as our fate, but one that we do not wish for ourselves and which we may yet choose to avoid (Dupuy, 2014). Having established the catastrophe's credibility we can begin by coming back to the present and think about what can be done in the here and now to ensure our survival. However, this reasoned optimism is undone if we continue to cling to the idea that science and technology will save us. Indeed, so long as we continue to convince ourselves that the solutions to our problems are just around the corner, we do not take the threat seriously. Even as catastrophe stares us in the face we cling desperately to hope. Half-heartedly we engage in various acts of pseudo-activity designed not to tackle the issues, but precisely to assuage our guilt in complicitly assaulting our own environment and those who occupy it.

Hope bred of false optimism is counterproductive (Hall & Winlow, 2007). As we have demonstrated here, hopelessness and the courage to confront it offer the best way out of our predicament. What *Inferno* and *The Day the Earth Stood Still* illustrate particularly well is that it is only when we are convinced that the end is *already here* are we willing to take the necessary steps to ensure our survival. To believe in catastrophe as fate is to prevent it from happening (Dupuy, 2013). Make no mistake, the pessimism of fatalism is nowhere to be found here. In exploring the realities of the world and constructing honest accounts of it, ultra-realism helps shine a light on the multitude of problems we face and attempts to tackle these head on (Winlow & Hall, 2019). This task can often seem a little bleak, but by adopting an approach that stresses an enlightened catastrophism ultra-realism engages in reasoned optimism. Disaster can be averted if we make the threat credible, accept it as our fate if we carry on as we are, and then, keeping this fate firmly locked in our sights, do all we can to block its realisation. As Robyn notes in Study-box 5 (see page 65), engaging in enlightened catastrophism can be a little depressing but it is certainly an important part of the ultra-realist arsenal, and one which can stimulate positive social change in contemporary society.

Study-box 5

Student Insight:

Meet Robyn, a 22-year-old undergraduate student.

Enlightened Catastrophism. Trust me it is not as scary as it sounds – however it might be a little depressing to learn. Despite this, I believe it to be a very insightful topic in relation to contemporary society. As a society we can't just sit around and fetishistically disavow the problems we are facing, expecting governments to one day finally see sense and make everything right. When reading about enlightened catastrophism I sometimes found the language very confusing. This made the reading hard to follow at first and the content became very overwhelming. To help with this I created a little glossary, this meant I didn't have to keep researching words because I forgot what they meant. It was always attached to my notes, always accessible and written in my own style making it easy to understand. If you need further explanation, do not be afraid to ask. This can be hard stuff; it may need to be explained more than once for it to sink in – this was the case for me.

Key Takeaway: Don't be afraid to ask 'silly' questions – they won't be silly, someone else will be thinking the same as you.

Study Questions:

- Why do we not take the threat of catastrophe seriously?
- Can you think of 3 examples of pseudo-activity and explain how they actively prevent real change?
- Why is it important to confront a zero point of hopelessness?

Key Reading: Winlow, S. (2017) 'The Uses of Catastrophism'. In Atkinson, R., McKenzie, L. and Winlow, S. (eds) *Building Better Societies: Promoting Social Justice in a World Falling Apart*, pp. 179-192. Bristol: Policy Press.

Fig. 5. Study-Box 5.

7

CONSUMER CULTURE, DESIRE AND LACK IN *FIGHT CLUB*

INTRODUCTION

The anticipation that surrounds the latest iPhone release or Black Friday deals are perhaps the most obvious examples that indicate we live in a consumer culture. According to estimates, UK consumers were expected to spend around £9 billion in the four days between Black Friday and Cyber Monday in 2021 (Davey, 2021). This comes against the backdrop of growing social inequality, a global pandemic where many lost jobs or required furlough payments at 80% of wage value, a supply chain crisis, growing food poverty and reduced welfare support. As an economic driver, consumer spending is critical (Horsley, 2015; Lloyd & Horsley, 2021); much of the early criticism of the lockdown policies during the COVID-19 pandemic focused on economic hardship and reduced spending, and much of the criticism of the removal of measures accused the government of caring more about consumer spending and the economy than public health (Briggs et al., 2020, 2021). From shopping, to online streaming, to social media, to holidays and travel, to nights out, consumer culture has colonised our leisure time; it is hard to identify leisure activities that are not opportunities to consume and spend (Raymen & Smith, 2019).

Bauman (2007) argued that we live 'consuming lives', and it is hard to argue with this statement. Consumerism also plays a significant part in the creation of identity and sense of self; the 'project of the self' is a work in progress whereby we can pick and choose who we want to be according to styles, tastes, fashions and cultural trends. When one identity no longer fits, we can pick another from the shelf and try again. This argument is often framed in positive tones – consumer culture in a postmodern world is liberating as we can be whoever we want to be (Miles, 1998). Others, such as Horkheimer and Adorno (1997), cautioned that the 'culture industry' was one of domination; something is provided for all so that none may escape. However, ultra-realist theory draws upon the Lacanian emphasis on lack and the structure of desire to understand why we remain in the grip of consumerism and why it remains ultimately unsatisfying. After all, what happens when we attain the commodity we've longed for? Usually, the novelty wears off and we want the next thing (see Study-box 6 (see page 77)).

As we saw in the previous chapter, and as recent work has demonstrated, consumerism can precipitate a range of harms that damage both our social and planetary well-being. Accordingly, as consumerism becomes more pervasive it is more important than ever to shine a criminological spotlight on it (Hall, Kuldova, & Horsley, 2020). In this chapter, we focus on Chuck Palahniuk's novel *Fight Club* and the David Fincher film adaptation to explore the inner workings of consumerism, lack, desire, drive and pleasure. Ultimately, the narrator shows us the dissatisfaction inherent with owning commodities. His search for something, anything, to address his lack propels him from consumerism to support groups, underground fighting and anarchist rebellion in a way that corresponds to the 'deviant leisure' perspective (Raymen & Smith, 2019). Let us explain how.

YOU TELL YOURSELF, 'THIS IS THE LAST SOFA I WILL EVER NEED IN MY LIFE'

Fight Club is ultimately a story of dissatisfaction. The narrator, a nameless, single, thirtysomething office worker, lives alone in his condominium, furnished via an IKEA catalogue. He suffers from insomnia and narcolepsy and appears to be drifting through life, attending support groups for testicular cancer, brain parasites, bone disease and dementia despite not suffering any of these diseases. He is clearly in search of something, and his introduction to Tyler Durden, a soap maker, acts as the catalyst for the events of the book and film. Tyler and our narrator form an underground fight club that writers such as Ta (2006) and Giroux (2001) suggest acts as a reflection of male violence and a patriarchal society. As the fight club develops, becomes popular and expands into other cities across the United States, it morphs into 'Project Mayhem', an organised revolt against the consumer capitalist system that has infantilised what Tyler refers to as "the middle children of history", enslaving them into the pursuit of consumer satisfaction and the low-paid service jobs that facilitate a consumer economy. Project Mayhem culminates in an act of terrorism whereby the headquarters of several credit card firms are blown up with homemade explosives; the slaves to consumer culture are set free through the eradication of credit card debt. By the end of the book and film, the narrator has come to the realisation that Tyler Durden is his own alter ego, or in Lacanian terms, his ego ideal. While *Fight Club* has been analysed along lines of patriarchy, male violence and the cultural contradictions of late capitalism (Lizardo, 2007), an ultra-realist interpretation draws from theoretical psychoanalysis to consider the relationship between lack, desire and consumerist ideology.

At the start of the film, the narrator is committed to the trappings of a consumer society. He decorates his condo via an IKEA catalogue while asking himself which dining set defines him as a person. Who he is as a person is defined by the things he owns; he projects an image of himself into the world based on the commodities he has bought and imbued with meaning:

> *When you buy furniture, you tell yourself, 'that's it, that's the last sofa I'm going to need. Whatever else happens, I've got the sofa problem handled'. I had it all. I had a stereo that was very decent, a wardrobe that was getting very respectable. I was close to being complete.*

The narrator conforms to the ideological exhortation at the centre of consumer culture: enjoy! (see Žižek, 2008). His accumulation of material possessions promises to make his life complete and bring ultimate satisfaction; he can derive fleeting pleasure from the meticulous construction of an identity based on the commodities that fill his life. His working life is mundane and unsatisfying, so he finds meaning in his consumer purchases; the post-industrial shift in identity-making away from one's occupation and towards one's leisure or consumer choices is apparent here (Lloyd, 2012).

Ultra-realist criminology has explored our attachment to consumer culture since its earliest forays into the milieus of criminal markets and the night-time economy (Hall, Winlow, & Ancrum, 2008; Smith, 2014; Winlow, 2001; Winlow & Hall, 2006). Treadwell, Briggs, Winlow, and Hall (2013) noted that some participants in the 2011 UK riots looted stores to acquire the money to then make legitimate purchases which would allow them to demonstrate their symbolic capital and inclusion within the competitive and status-driven world of consumer culture. The deviant leisure perspective pioneered by Thomas Raymen and Oliver Smith (see Raymen, 2019b; Raymen & Smith, 2016, 2019, 2020; Smith, 2014; Smith & Raymen, 2017), and underpinned by ultra-realist theory (Winlow, 2019), shows how harmful and 'deviant' behaviour such as Black Friday 'shopping with violence' or lifestyle gambling represents conformity to the tenets of consumer capitalism, and not a deviation from societal norms and values. Neoliberal capitalist ideology exhorts the competitive individual to be all they can be, to rise above the herd and stand out, to display their success for everyone to see (Hall et al., 2008). Ultimately, we think this achievement and success will bring us satisfaction. However, as the narrator in *Fight Club* shows us, this is not the case and we must dig further; insights from theoretical psychoanalysis can help us make sense of dissatisfaction, lack and desire.

LACK, DESIRE AND LIBIDINAL ENERGY

Why are we attached to consumer culture? Why are some people willing to inflict harm on others in pursuit of the trappings of consumer 'success'? Ultra-realism suggests that criminological or sociological theory that places emphasis on the individual agent's freedom of choice or the pressure to conform or 'keep up with the Joneses' misses the powerful role of the unconscious and requires a re-evaluation of the nature of subjectivity (see Chapter 3). The transcendental materialist subject is characterised by lack (Hall, 2012a). The subject is 'split' at the point of emergence into the world; in order to live in the world we each give up an essential part of our being and pass from a state of nature, or raw drive, into a state of culture (Freud, 2003; Hall, 2012a). On an unconscious level, the split subject is driven to act and attempt to undo that fundamental split. We are constantly in search of the 'lost' object, what Lacan refers to as *objet a*; the thing that will make us whole again and lead to satisfaction. This means the subject is a *desiring subject*, conceived by lack and compelled to act in search of wholeness or satisfaction. In our subconscious, we know something is missing.

As discussed in Chapter 3, the transcendental materialist subject must solicit a Symbolic Order to avoid confrontation with the Real. The void of subjectivity must be filled by a set of signs, symbols, norms and ways of being and, increasingly, that Symbolic Order is one that emphasises competition, individualism, status, display and the delights of consumer culture. That Symbolic Order also tells us that our identity is mutable, that we have the freedom to change and are not constrained by anything. Economically, consumerism is central to Western economies and so the desiring subject must become a consuming subject (Hall et al., 2008). When that ideological imperative grafts onto the split-subject's pursuit of the lost object, a powerful libidinal drive is directed into consumer markets (Raymen & Smith, 2019). We believe we can satisfy that lack through our latest purchases or experiences in commodified leisure spaces. But we already know this isn't the case. Think about your most recent consumer purchase: you desired it, wanted it, got excited at the thought of acquiring it but how long did it take for the novelty to wear off? And what did you do next? Move on to the next object of desire. The next thing that will make you whole and bring ultimate satisfaction. We are compelled by our subjective lack to jump back into the marketplace in the hope that the next big night out or shopping trip or online order will bring happiness. Todd McGowan (2016) is surely right to suggest that capitalism's harnessing of subjective desire ties the individual to the economic system and propels us into an endless process of searching for satisfaction.

When we return to the narrator in *Fight Club*, the previous quotation shows us his deep commitment to consumer culture; the IKEA catalogue becomes the means to fill the void but, in Lacanian terms, the object of desire keeps shifting. The sofa doesn't satisfy him so he thinks the stereo will. Or the wardrobe. Or the dining set. His belief that he was close to being complete is, of course, fantasy. His insomnia and obvious dissatisfaction at the start of the film demonstrates this. All this stuff does not fill up the void, does not make him happy and does not remove the nagging sense that something is missing. The 'lost object' exists beyond the pleasure principle and he senses this; the consumer goods he purchases represent a series of stand-in objects that cannot bring satisfaction. In the story, the narrator fails to achieve his 'complete' life through an act of self-sabotage; his flat is destroyed in what we initially believe to be a gas leak but later find, through Tyler Durden, that the narrator was responsible for the explosion. Following McGowan (2016), the narrator believes he is close to satisfaction and therefore destroyed the flat in order to delay satisfaction precisely because its absence, and the *promise* of attaining it, is the ultimate source of satisfaction. Yet, on an unconscious level he realises that consumer purchases will not make him complete, will not achieve his search for fulfilment or meaning and will not erase the sense that something is missing.

Before the arrival of Tyler Durden and the birth of the fight club, the narrator uses support groups as his first attempt to find meaning beyond consumer culture. The authentic emotional connections made through support groups for men with testicular cancer or those suffering with blood parasites provide a sense of release and allow him to sleep. Although he is a fraud or 'tourist', he feels seen by other people in a way that he lacks elsewhere. Marla, another 'tourist', symbolically castrates him by reflecting his own lie back on him and his insomnia returns. In the novel, the narrator explains why the support groups mattered:

> *If people thought you were dying, they gave you their full attention. If this might be the last time they saw you, they really saw you. Everything else about their checkbook balance and radio songs and messy hair went out the window. You had their full attention. People listened instead of just waiting for their turn to speak. And when they spoke, they weren't telling you a story. When the two of you talked, you were building something, and afterward you were both different than before.*
>
> *(Palahniuk, 1996/2006, p. 107)*

This is a clear representation of what Badiou (2005) calls a 'passion for the real'; a zealous desire for something in the moment, in the here and now. The narrator is searching for authentic connection and experience and finds it in support groups. But it is built on a lie. It is an interesting indictment of modern culture that Palahniuk believes the consumer-subject can only find true connection and meaning in extreme circumstances and through deception. Outside of support groups for the dying, there is too much background noise and subjective commitment to consumer ideology to find 'real' meaningful interaction. Marla shatters the illusion, and he has to look elsewhere for authenticity and the chance to feel alive. Enter Tyler Durden and the fight club. Tyler points out that the things we own end up owning us and that our engagement with consumer culture is a futile pursuit with no chance of satisfaction:

> *God dammit, an entire generation pumping gas, waiting tables. Slaves with white collars. Advertising has us chasing cars and clothes, working jobs we hate so we can buy shit we don't need.*

Tyler is articulating the decline of symbolic efficiency (Winlow & Hall, 2013). The fundamental lack at the heart of the subject can no longer be 'filled up' with the Symbolic Order's meanings, signs, symbols and identities; the consuming subject, heeding the superego's injunction to 'enjoy!', can find no satisfaction in the substitute objects originally signposted as the route to fulfilment or in the identity created around a consumer lifestyle. Winlow and Hall (2006), Smith (2014) and Ellis et al. (2018) all show how the imperative to consume propels young men and women into the night-time economy, searching for the excitement of the 'big night out'. These studies all interview participants who actually reveal the disappointment and failure of the shiny consumer spectacle; their hedonistic abandon fails to live up to the anticipation and the subjects often see through the façade. However, they are back the next week or next year, still chasing the illusion. The narrator has already sensed this lack and dissatisfaction and sought alternative avenues only for Marla to break the spell. Tyler offers a new way to fill the void.

THE FIRST RULE OF FIGHT CLUB IS YOU DO NOT TALK ABOUT CONFORMITY

Fight club allows its members to feel alive. This also represents Badiou's 'passion for the real' as the fights are physical, intimate, immediate and require the participant to be present. The roar of the crowd and the physical sensations in the moment allow the subject to filter out the drudgery of the working week and the dissatisfaction in other parts of their lives. They have tested themselves and shown themselves to be up to the challenge. They have purpose, belonging and an outlet for their libidinal energy and drive. Lacan refers to *jouissance* as the excess of pleasure that can be unsettling or bring a degree of pain; the actual physical pain associated with the satisfaction derived from fight club demonstrates that the participants may have turned away from consumer capitalism but are still subjects of lack and desire. Satisfying that desire moves the subject into the realm of *jouissance*. The deviant leisure perspective argues that more extreme behaviours in the pursuit of enjoyment in consumer or leisure activity represents a parasuicidal disregard for life and well-being (Raymen & Smith, 2019). Although seemingly rejecting the imperatives of consumer capitalism, fight club, in its early formation, is essentially a leisure activity. Returning to fight club on a weekly basis to take (and give) a physical beating is a clear reflection of Raymen and Smith's parasuicidal form of leisure. Their quest for satisfaction and enjoyment is so extreme that they are willing to risk serious injury in its pursuit.

Within ultra-realist research, numerous forms of parasuicidal leisure and consumption have been researched, from parkour and free running (Raymen, 2019b), hedonistic bouts of alcohol consumption (Ellis et al., 2018; Smith, 2014), online gambling (Raymen & Smith, 2020) and steroid use (Kotzé, Richardson, & Antonopoulos, 2020). The willingness to risk harm to the self and others in the pursuit of enjoyment is visible in many hyper-conformist leisure activities. Fight club is the epitome of this *jouissance* and para-suicidal enjoyment. The compulsive, repetitive element of these behaviours raises the spectre of death drive. In fact, it is fair to say the story is one of death drive; the repetitive compulsion to act in destructive ways in order to complete the symbolic annihilation of an identity forged in a consumer capitalist culture that will not provide the enjoyment or satisfaction the subject seeks. Following Tyler's injunction that "it's only after we've lost everything that we're free to do anything", the narrator systematically and repeatedly destroys his identity in order to create himself anew. He blows up his flat, leaves his job, changes his name, opens a fight club, leads a terrorist organisation, before ultimately shooting himself in the head. Before fight club, he tries on alternative identities through the pseudonyms he adopts at support groups but none of them stick, at least until Tyler.

> *I love everything about Tyler Durden, his courage and his smarts. His nerve. Tyler is funny and charming and forceful and independent, and men look up to him and expect him to change their world. Tyler is capable and free, and I am not.*
>
> *(Palahniuk, 1996/2006, p. 174)*

Tyler Durden is the narrator's ego ideal; his imaginary ideal version of who he wants to be. He feels sorry for men who religiously go to the gym and sculpt their bodies in ways that correspond to the male models in underwear adverts, yet his ego ideal looks like Brad Pitt. For all his opposition to the status and display associated with consumer capitalism, his ideal self is one who does succeed on those terms. Tyler is handsome, successful and free: women want to be with him and men want to be him. He is a leader and inspires devotion in the other lost souls looking for belonging. By all measures, he is a winner in a consumer capitalist society divided into winners and losers. Kotzé and Antonopoulos (2021) argue that use of steroids and other Image and Performance Enhancing Drugs (IPEDs) reflect the body as a site of pleasurable aesthetic consumption. Moreover, a primed and tuned body also possesses significant instrumental utility that can be put to work in various ways. The upshot is that in helping to attain a suitably sculpted and instrumentally effective physique, steroids essentially boost bodily capital that acts as a signal of success, power and strength to others. Rather than a deviant act, the attachment to sculpted 'Insta-ready' physiques represents further conformity to neoliberalism's core cultural norms and values. It also represents the lack at the heart of subjectivity; the perfect physique is mistakenly viewed as a way to satisfy the desire that springs from lack. Perhaps it is no surprise, then, that the narrator's ego ideal is Brad Pitt.

Tyler Durden also represents Hall's (2012a) criminal undertaker, emboldened by special liberty, who goes out into the world and acts because he can; someone has to show the credit card companies, the bosses, the people who keep the servant class down, and he's the one to do it. As with the forms of deviant leisure outlined by Raymen, Smith and others, Tyler Durden and fight club are hyper-conformist, despite their anarchist and underground intentions. The structuring fantasy at the heart of consumer capitalism is that we live in a liquid society where everything, right down to our very identity and sense of self, is flexible and open to change if required. If you don't like who you are, you can reinvent yourself. Tyler Durden is the narrator's attempt to reinvent himself through an ego ideal that reflects the epitome of success within neoliberal consumer capitalism whilst rejecting the identities sold to us by a system that equates 'stuff' with happiness and selfhood.

It is tempting to read *Fight Club* as non-conformist. The narrator rejects consumer capitalism in favour of underground fighting and terrorism. The film version offers a clear and strong critique of the vacuity and meaningless nature of addiction to the status and display associated with a consumer identity. Tyler Durden's soap company makes soap from reconstituted human fat, stolen from liposuction clinics and sold back to high-end department stores for profit. Consumer capitalism creates desire for perfect bodies that we can show off to others, signal our success and ostensibly fulfil our fundamental lack, but by selling our own waste back to us as an expensive and fashionable commodity we see the problems of ideology and the impact on the subject. However, what *Fight Club* actually represents is hyper-conformity (Kotzé, 2019; Raymen & Smith, 2019). The narrator's quest for a 'successful' identity forces a compulsive process of self-annihilation. The lack at the core of his subjectivity is harnessed as desire by a consumer capitalist ideology that sets him on a destructive search for satisfaction. What *Fight Club* does reveal is that satisfaction and enjoyment are found beyond the pleasure principle: the trappings of commodities and status are fleeting and unsustainable. Far from offering a sense of completeness, the freedom to change oneself and try on multiple selves and identities creates ontological insecurity (Hall, 2012a).

CONCLUSION

At the end of *Fight Club*, the narrator abandons the political terrorism of Project Mayhem for a human connection with Marla. It is telling that, in the end, the narrator rejects Tyler in favour of Marla. Badiou (2012) argues that love is one of the keys to a fulfilling life – not the pursuit of pleasure and enjoyment. We could question whether the ending shows the narrator moving 'beyond the pleasure principle'. It is interesting that the critique of consumer capitalism and its effect on dissatisfied subjects finds its expression in *Fight Club* and ultimately manifests as anti-capitalist terrorism. Mark Fisher's

(2009) suggestion that it's easier to imagine the end of the world than the end of capitalism comes into focus here. We could argue that *Fight Club* is reflective of capitalist realism: the search for enjoyment beyond consumer capitalism inevitably leads to bombings and terror. Do we have to blow it all up to start again? As we saw in Chapter 6, staring into the abyss offers revelation, and an enlightened catastrophism provides the opportunity to determine the level of intervention required to step back from the brink.

What *Fight Club* shows us is the deep connection between subjective lack and desire, the ideology of consumer capitalism and the drive of libidinal energy. We seek to fill the void with replacement objects and experiences which often only provide fleeting satisfaction before we turn our attention to the next thing, and the next thing. The disquieting feeling at the back of our minds tells us that satisfaction and enjoyment will not be satiated through consumer goods. The transcendental materialist subject is, however, characterised by lack, and therefore desire is the force that propels us to act in the world and seek out a way to achieve that subjective satisfaction and make us whole again. In a culture dominated by the imperatives of consumer capitalism, that desire, that libidinal energy, is directed towards the economic demands of consumption. In the wake of *Fight Club's* cultural impact, real-life fight clubs sprang up around the world. These fight clubs are much more commercialised, shiny, commodified versions than those in the film; showing us yet again how consumer capitalism successfully incorporates its critique into new marketable commodities.

Fight Club is a story of the dissatisfaction found in consumer culture and the search for alternative ways to find meaning and enjoyment. The narrator, through Tyler Durden, turns to a parasuicidal form of leisure that causes as much harm as it does satisfaction. No matter how badly beaten, how many broken teeth or bones, how many stitches, the compulsion of death drive forces him and others back into a harmful form of leisure. It is also a story of hyper-conformity; no matter how much the narrator protests against the meaningless nature of consumer culture or the negative impact it has had on the consuming subject, the structure of desire locks him into the repetitive search for enjoyment and this search takes place within the ideological confines of the dominant Symbolic Order. The narrator heeds the postmodern edict to be free, to cast off unwanted or spoiled identities and make himself anew. Tyler Durden represents liberation and freedom from the rules and conformity, embodying what ultra-realism would describe as 'special liberty'. However, while he might not follow the legal rules, Tyler Durden is still playing on the ideological field of neoliberal capitalism and his desire is shaped and directed accordingly.

Study-box 6

Student Insight:

Meet Lauren, a 22-year-old undergraduate student.

Ultra-realism is definitely a difficult topic to get stuck into, but I found ways to make it easier. One was to apply the topic to real-life events that were personal to me, something I could relate to. For example, with desire and lack, it was very easy to understand just by looking at my own feelings around getting something new, like a phone or laptop. It was something I worked hard for and really wanted, but as soon as I had it, the shiny new thing became part of life and I moved on. It wasn't exciting anymore. This is how lack and desire fuel capitalism; we are always after the next thing. More generally, I cannot emphasise enough how important it is to read. There is so much out there on the topic to help you along. Make notes, ask questions, read more. Ultra-realism is a really interesting topic, and one that has even made me look at my own behaviours with regards to lack, desire and consumption, and how I engage with capitalism through its manufactured 'micro-revolutions'. It is a thought-provoking subject for sure and although ultra-realism can be quite intimidating to approach, do not let that put you off.

Key Takeaway: Read plenty and don't be afraid to ask questions.

Study Questions:

- How does lack and desire explain our attachment to consumer culture?
- How does the deviant leisure perspective change our view of deviance and conformity?
- Can you think of other examples where lack and desire is visible in a film or TV series?

Key Reading: Raymen, T. and Smith, O. (2019) 'Deviant Leisure: A Critical Criminological Perspective for the Twenty-first Century', *Critical Criminology*, 27 (1), pp. 115-130.

Fig. 6. Study-Box 6.

8

VIOLENCE, TRAUMA AND *RAY DONOVAN*

INTRODUCTION

We have already questioned and offered some explanation as to why some people willingly inflict harm on others. Here, we ask a more specific question: how and why are some people more attuned than others to the rhythms, textures and meanings of extreme forms of violence? As we outlined in Chapter 2, aetiology and causation are marginal interests within mainstream criminology and often generate concerns about pathologising the individual offender (Gadd & Jefferson, 2007; Winlow, 2014). Still, the popular fascination with violence and violent subjectivity populates our TV screens and our reading material; Wattis (2021) outlines the popularity of the 'hardman' genre of true crime literature. From the Kray twins to Tony Soprano, we remain fascinated by violent men which returns us to the question above. However, real encounters, with violent subjects in pubs, on housing estates, in our daily lives, are often more troublesome and far less glamorous. Ultra-realist criminology has a long-standing history of exploring violence and masculinity (Ellis, 2016; Ellis, Winlow, & Hall, 2017; Hall, 1997; Winlow, 2001, 2014; Winlow & Hall, 2006) and has increasingly focused on a specific population of violent men informed by a complex combination of trauma, biography and background or upbringing. In this chapter, we explore these factors through the world of Showtime's US TV series *Ray Donovan*. Across the show's seven seasons, the complexity of the title character, played by Liev Schrieber, unfolds in a way that illustrates the development of an ultra-realist theory of violence, from the instrumental and entrepreneurial use of violence as a commodity (Winlow, 2001) to the psychosocial, Lacanian informed consideration of shame, humiliation and guilt (Ellis et al., 2017; Winlow & Hall, 2009), to the deep-seated role of trauma in violent biography (Winlow, 2014). We compare

Ray to his brother 'Bunchy' and draw on other examples including the fictional – Tony Soprano – and the real – Lenny McLean.

SITUATING VIOLENT MEN

When we first meet Ray Donovan, we find a working-class Boston-Irish man in his early 40s transplanted into the glamorous world of Los Angeles and Hollywood. He works as a 'fixer' for a law firm that represents celebrity clients and heads of film studios. Ray represents the Real behind the Symbolic Order of Hollywood. The glamorous image of opulence, wealth and creativity has an ugly underside; the executives are heartless crooks, the stars are selfish, addicted and troubled, and Ray's job is to ensure this glamorous veneer remains intact. His violence is the frequent irruption of the Real that shows us the limits of Hollywood's ideology. On the surface, Ray Donovan represents the ego ideal of hegemonic masculinity; he is physically fit, imposing, well dressed, drives a nice car, lives in a big house with his wife and children, appears financially secure and is successful in his chosen career. He is also, when called upon, capable of handling himself adeptly and is skilled in the use of violence. When compared with his brothers – Terry, a physically broken, Parkinson's-ridden ex-boxer and 'Bunchy', a mentally broken child sexual abuse victim with serious addiction problems, Ray is thriving. He has made successful entrepreneurial use of his propensity for violence and his willingness to transgress legal codes (Winlow, 2001). However, he also cheats on his wife, exposes his children to his violence and drinks excessively to numb an as-yet-unidentified pain. As the series progresses, he also enacts extreme violence, up to and including murder, on numerous occasions.

His tough working-class upbringing, further sculpted through exposure to the worlds of boxing and various forms of petty and organized crime, have provided Ray with an appreciation and understanding of the utility and language of violence (Winlow, 2001; Winlow & Hall, 2009). He has clearly commodified his propensity for violence and found entrepreneurial utility in its instrumental use. We could say he represents the neoliberal injunction to maximise his human capital and succeed in a competitive marketplace, but he also represents what Hall (2012a) refers to as a 'criminal undertaker'; he's the guy you call to get shit done. In line with Winlow's (2001) analysis of working-class men, once destined for heavy industry and durable forms of masculine-dominated work, who translated their 'visceral habitus' (Hall, 1997) into a business opportunity within emerging criminal markets, Ray is valuable (and successful) in terms of solving problems outside of the restricted confines of the law. In the early episodes, his violence is almost always instrumental and in the service of his business interests. He also has a reputation within his industry that clearly precedes him; he has been successfully taking care of business in his own unique way for some time. However, the opening premise of the story is the unexpected return of his father, Mickey Donovan, after 20 years in prison. The impact of Mickey's return on Ray signals an increase in his use of expressive, rather than instrumental, violence and forces us to look deeper for ways to make sense of his actions.

A BACKGROUND OF VIOLENCE

Winlow (2014, p. 35) moves beyond meta-psychology of psychopathy or sociopathy as well as pathologising violent men to connect "the deep traumas of internal life to the social field that shapes those traumas and determines the context of their return". The ultra-realist exploration of violent subjectivity focuses on a small sample of men and is not necessarily a general theory of violence. However, given that most violence is enacted by a small percentage of the population who are also more likely to be victims of violence themselves (Ellis, 2016; Hall, 2012a), it is critical we understand what fuels this violence. In the final episode of season 1, Mickey admonishes Ray:

> *You know what your problem is, Ray? You cling to the past. You need to move on.*

In attempting to understand his son's actions – which in this season includes orchestrating an attempt on Mickey's life – Mickey makes an analytical error: Ray does not cling to his past, his past clings to him. What past does Mickey refer to? Ray and his brother Bunchy were both sexually abused as young boys by their parish priest. We learn that 10-year-old Ray told his father, who accused Ray of lying and then badly beat him. Ray's mother dies of cancer when the children are young; Mickey was with his mistress while his wife died. Ray's younger sister, Bridget, commits suicide as a teenager after being raped by the local gangster who has taken Ray under his wing. Mickey is also an abusive parent who encouraged Ray to box but would 'beat the shit' out of him if he lost. In short, he is raised in an environment where toughness and violence are firmly embedded cultural codes, and traumatic events are littered throughout Ray's formative years.

The violent subject internalises childhood experiences of trauma, biography and external environment in ways that shape the internal psyche, the relationship to violence and sense of self (Ellis, 2016; Winlow, 2014). Violence itself is valued but, perhaps more important, is the ability to retain a sense of dignity and respect in the face of violence; "'looking after' oneself and 'refusing to take shit' have become, for some men at least, compelling strategies internalized by the habitus" (Winlow & Hall, 2009, p. 288). The background and environment in which men like Ray are raised are crucial. Those codes and values are internalised by the subject. There is a deep, complex and rich internal life at the heart of the violent subject that encompasses a range of powerful emotions: rage, shame, humiliation and guilt are all dynamic components which inform both self-identity and responses to events, both real and imagined, in the present.

Parental influence in the shaping of masculinity is crucial here (Winlow, 2014; Winlow & Hall, 2009). Several examples are illustrative. In the first episode, upon hearing of Mickey's release from prison and intention to join his family in Los Angeles, Ray warns his wife Abby to keep Mickey away from his children:

Ray: *"Whatever you think happened, it was ten times worse. Don't let the wolf in the gate".*

Abby: *"You're sick, Ray. You've got a hole in your heart".*

Both characters are correct. Ray is right that Mickey is a narcissistic, violent, predatory monster. Abby is also correct in saying that Ray is broken, but she lacks the insight to understand why; the combination of an abusive father, unresolved childhood trauma, biography and his background have all contributed to Ray's subjectivity. We then turn to Ray's relationship to his teenage son, Conor. During a family visit to a school open day, Conor hits another boy for making fun of him. When Abby punishes Conor, he phones his Dad to complain but Ray cuts him off:

> *When you hit someone in the head, there are consequences. Be a man and deal with it.*

This injunction to a form of stoic masculinity represents a process of 'toughening up' that encourages Conor to move away from childish things and learn to deal with the cold, hard reality of a world that will cut him no slack (Winlow, 2014). Interestingly, Ray seems to sense the problematic impact of this approach on Conor and phones him back but is immediately cut off by a knock at the door. We later learn that this is how Mickey raised his children and we see numerous examples of Mickey's appalling parenting 'style' throughout the show. In the next episode, Ray's drive to keep Mickey from his children's lives takes a violent turn. Bunchy's housewarming party goes horribly wrong, and Ray finds his children have attended against his wishes. Conor is both drunk and high, thanks to Mickey, and Ray arrives to take them home. When Ray gets angry at Conor, Mickey shows us his own brand of parenting, goading Ray:

> *You're mad at me, fine, but he's just a kid. Sorry I didn't go to more of your football games.*

He is subtly insinuating that Ray's anger reflects his 'soft' character; he needed handholding as a child in a way that Mickey probably didn't. Ray is, in effect, not a 'real' man. Ray responds by pistol whipping Mickey in front of his children, pointing a gun at his head and traumatising his children in the process. It represents the first real demonstration of expressive violence (Wieviorka, 2009); the 'red mist' or rage that Ellis (2016) and Winlow (2014) both describe has descended, he's not fully in control and he's driven by feelings of shame and humiliation. As Winlow (2014, p. 37) notes: "These men know the destructive power they possess, and they know that this power has the capacity to destroy sources of nourishment and value in their everyday lives".

The environment in which Ray was raised, involving violence, a process of 'toughening up' and the value placed on particular forms of durable and stoic masculinity, not only shapes Ray's subjectivity but the internalisation of these experiences and values returns in problematic ways. Ray's failure to deal with violent incidents in his childhood, including regular beatings from his father, becomes lodged in his memory and the emotions associated with his failure to act or protect himself, likely guilt, shame and humiliation, not only inform his habitus and self-identity (Winlow & Hall, 2009) but also inform his actions when those feelings return in Mickey's presence. The calculating instrumental violence we see Ray employ in his job disappears and the impulsive, expressive violence driven by these emotions is activated, regardless of consequence.

We can momentarily move from Ray Donovan into true crime memoirs for other examples. Wattis (2021) notes that the 'hard man' genre of literature can provide insights into violence and masculinity. In his bestselling memoir *The Guv'nor*, published just before his death in 1998, Lenny McLean chronicles his journey from the impoverished post-war East End of London, through unlicenced boxing, nightclub door management, to film stardom in Guy Ritchie's *Lock, Stock and Two Smoking Barrels*. If we follow Winlow (2014) and Ellis (2016) and see violent masculinity emerge from childhood trauma, upbringing and environment, McLean is a useful example. Born in the East End of London in 1949 in a rough working-class neighbourhood, McLean grew up in an environment of tough, durable masculinity, where a willingness to step outside of legal regulations and an appreciation of the codes and utility of violence were commonplace. McLean was also physically abused by his stepfather who would beat him and his mother.

McLean talks about the shame and humiliation of being physically dominated by a grown man and of not being able to protect his mother. This trauma, alongside a social and cultural understanding of violence, propelled McLean into violent encounters for most of the remainder of his life. He became a bare knuckle and unlicenced fighter, a street brawler, a nightclub bouncer and a petty criminal, steadily building upon a formidable reputation for extreme and explosive violence. He articulates an inability to back down from a challenge, echoing Winlow and Hall (2009) and Ellis et al. (2017) who suggest that the psychic shame and humiliation of *not* fighting would be too traumatic to bear. McLean was forced to back down by his abusive stepfather, and he would never do it again. In some respects, the violence he faced throughout his life are encounters with the same foe, over and over. Beneath a tough exterior is a tangled web of insecurities and structuring anxiety that resides in the unconscious (Winlow, 2014). He can't let anything challenge his self-identity and risk symbolic annihilation, he can't risk the shame and humiliation wrought upon him as a child resurfacing; he must act, and act violently. He identified his stepfather as a bully who only stopped after McLean, once he became physically capable of standing up to the challenge, confronted him. Anyone he regarded as a bully became a symbolic stand-in and had to be dealt with; as Winlow (2014, p. 36) argues, he "must continually face down bullies and tormentors in the same way they did during their youth". He is Hall's 'criminal undertaker' who takes it upon himself to right the wrongs. He knows how it feels to be bullied, shamed, humiliated, and those traumatic emotions are unconsciously activated through his social and cultural understanding of violence.

Returning to Ray Donovan, we can momentarily consider the role of the 'criminal undertaker' (Hall, 2012a). Essentially, this is a subject of special liberty (see Chapter 4). The sovereign individual rises above the herd and takes control *because someone must*. If that requires them to step outside of legal or moral codes to do what needs to be done, so be it. After Bunchy confronts the priest who abused him, Ray murders the priest when he reveals that Ray was also abused. Terry, a devout catholic, sees this act as a mortal sin but Ray's response is simple: they did what had to be done. The rules don't apply, the law doesn't apply. Something needed to be done and he shouldered the burden to do it. We can see this in another popular TV anti-hero, Tony Soprano in HBO's classic, *The Sopranos*. In one storyline, the school football coach is revealed to be sexually abusing a teenage girl on the team. As many of the main characters have daughters at the school, they are outraged and demand justice. Tony decides that the justice system will not provide appropriate retribution and decides to settle matters himself. When his childhood friend Artie, a civilian and not part of the crime family, asks Tony to call off his own retribution, Tony replies:

> *What do you want to do Artie? Call the cops? Here's the phone. They'll arrest him, right? And he'll be out in two fuckin' years and he'll move up to Saskatchewan and you know what he'll do? He'll teach girls soccer and he'll start all over again.*

We cannot rely on our institutions to protect our children or provide justice so Tony, as the criminal undertaker, is required to act. In the end, Tony does call it off and the coach is arrested. However, Tony's internal turmoil at not enacting his special liberty takes its toll; the episode ends with him returning home, incredibly drunk, and before he passes out, he tells his wife, "I didn't hurt no-one". He knows he has done the right thing but in doing so he has acted against his own internal compulsion; his drinking to excess is an attempt to obliterate the shame of *not acting*. There are clearly powerful emotions at work in the violence undertaken by these characters.

MAKING SENSE OF TRAUMA

This final section returns to *Ray Donovan* to delve deeper into the role of trauma. It is worth noting that the show does deviate from the ultra-realist theory on violent subjectivity in different ways. First, Winlow and Hall (2009) suggest that feelings of humiliation and shame make it impossible for violent men to back down or ignore real or perceived threats to their sense of self. Ellis (2016) also indicates that his participants were unable to back down or walk away from the inevitability of a violent situation that must be dealt with. Ray can walk away, and he does on numerous occasions, without any apparent impact on his psyche. Challenges to his image and sense of self appear to leave no feelings of guilt or insecurity. However, when we start to look at the impact of violent events in his past, Ray and his brothers do correspond to the ultra-realist theory of violence. A deeper understanding of the role of trauma opens our discussion further.

> *The child who is socialized in a micro-climate of insecurity and fear, and subject to an external cultural field that encourages tough masculinity, will often encounter deeply traumatic events that resonate throughout his adult life. The subject will return to these events countless times as the psyche attempts to deal with the emotional pain they inspire. In many cases the actuality of traumatic events cannot be revisited in a straightforward manner. The events themselves were so injurious that conscious recollection would be far too painful for the psyche to bear. In such cases they are disguised by the psyche's various defence systems. The 'memory' of the traumatic event takes a different form, or it is shut away, disavowed or repressed. However, the repressed memory inevitably returns as the psyche attempts to cathartically release the disturbing energy of the traumatic event.*
>
> *(Winlow, 2014, p. 42)*

This long quotation leads us towards examination of the way in which the psyche deals with traumatic experience, how the subject remembers those events and how the energy created by traumatic memory impacts upon behaviour in the present. Following the work of Christopher Bollas (1995), the foundation of human relations is built upon elemental trust. Children 'trust' their parents to defend and nurture them, and the breakdown of this trust is detrimental to the child's psychic well-being (Winlow, 2014). This forces an encounter with the Lacanian Real. When Ray explains to Mickey why he tried to have him killed, he demonstrates the traumatic impact of the breakdown in elemental trust. Ray reveals he told Mickey about his sexual abuse and was accused of lying and badly beaten. Instead of the parent defending and nurturing his child, providing the symbolic reassurance to turn away from the traumatic Real, Mickey broke that trust in a traumatic way; Ray acknowledges that his father has been symbolically dead to him since he was 10 years old. Ellis (2016) describes how Bollas (1995) uses the analogy of Little Red Riding Hood to accentuate this point. The wolf *appears* as a comforting figure, the unthreatening granny wrapped in a bonnet and a blanket but reveals itself to be the wolf lying in wait, ready to claim its victim. The moment of revelation and realisation is unsettling, traumatic and incomprehensible. Ray Donovan appears as a reader of Bollas: his warning to Abby in the first episode is to *not let the wolf in the gate*. The combination of his sexual abuse and the parental destruction of trust have inscribed trauma on Ray's psyche.

The relationship between trauma and guilt also plays a significant role in understanding violent subjectivity. Guilt is ultimately unconscious. According to Žižek (2000), the subject is either unaware of their guilt or does experience guilt but is unclear about what they feel guilty for. On a conscious level, the victim of childhood trauma or abuse may feel no guilt about their victimhood but unconsciously these feelings are crucial in the development of their psychopathology. Of course, the victim of such abuse has no reason to feel guilt; they were defenceless children. However, Johnston and Malabou (2013) instruct us that the conscious feeling – anxiety or shame, for example – may be a 'misfelt' feeling of unconscious guilt. Unconsciously, the adult may come to believe that his younger self somehow caused, wanted or even enjoyed the traumatic experience; the experience of victimhood is shameful, not because there is anything to be ashamed of, but because it is thought that the child – the younger self – somehow provoked the violence.

Bunchy, for example, talks to Abby about his sexual abuse and says that he thought he wanted it to happen. What Bunchy reveals here is the workings of the unconscious fantasy space behind the subjective self-identity (Winlow, 2014). Lacan's *jouissance* refers to pleasure-seeking that results in pain, self-sabotage or an unsettling revelation that the subject would have preferred to remain hidden. Our fantasy space is not fully rational, but when the gap closes between internal fantasy and social identity, the result may be traumatic. The shame he feels is not because he has been victimised but because his victimisation indirectly touches on the content of his fantasy. This is not to say that Bunchy *wanted* his abuse but instead that he somehow feels he *caused* it. Bunchy does appear to feel conscious shame, but Ray does not. Shame, for Ray, is an unconscious affect created by traumatic experiences that work in the background to shape the way in which he engages with social life. It is a 'misfelt' feeling that drives him, fuels both his expressive and instrumental violence, and keeps others at arm's length. Mickey's return allows these feelings to resurface, and in his increasingly violent and destructive response, we catch sight of his shame.

The difference in response between Ray and Bunchy is critically important. This trauma-informed theory of violent subjectivity does not imply that traumatic childhood experience mechanistically *causes* violence in later life. Nor does it say that violence is a direct expression of childhood trauma. What it *does* imply is that childhood trauma, an environment characterised by specific gendered socialisation and a cultural appreciation for violence are crucial elements in understanding how some violent subjects are formed. As we see with Ray and Bunchy, both are violent in different ways, both are self-destructive, but both have significant degrees of agency to act in the world. Their similar backgrounds and upbringings have given them both a cultural appreciation for violence, a willingness to utilise it where necessary and both are driven, in different ways, by unconscious feelings of shame, guilt and humiliation. However, Ray has found entrepreneurial use for his violent subjectivity, has raised a family and become, on the surface, successful. Although a similar age, Bunchy is more childlike, has difficulty holding down a job, is sexually dysfunctional and unable to maintain relationships, is drug and alcohol addicted and more reliant on others. The ways in which their trauma, biography and environments shape and influence their actions show both the role of unconscious feelings and the role of agency in understanding their violence.

CONCLUSION

Mainstream criminology has moved away from attempting to understand violence (Hall & Winlow, 2015). However, given the harms caused by violent behaviour – to the victim *and* the offender – it is critical that theories of violence develop and progress. Traumatic childhood experience does not mechanistically *cause* violence in later life. It is also not sufficient to propel the individual into violent behaviour. The individual also requires a gendered socialisation that stresses toughness, physicality and a stoic outlook. The traumatised individual must also be encouraged to value violence (Ellis et al., 2017). Not all men are violent and not all violent men correspond to the theory of violence outlined in this chapter. Ultra-realist criminology, particularly through the work of Simon Winlow and Anthony Ellis, has tried to capture the psychosocial factors behind a small group of particularly violent men. By looking at the characters in *Ray Donovan*, we can see how childhood trauma, background and biography can inform a subjective relationship to violence that is apparent on cultural, social and psychological levels. Some men are willing to inflict serious harm on others and accept the likelihood of serious harm to the self. They often accept this stoically as a price worth paying to avoid painful feelings of shame, humiliation or guilt. The fictional Ray Donovan's violence is both instrumental and expressive and while he has marketised his propensity for violence and willingness to step outside the law where necessary, he is also driven by feelings of guilt and shame. The real-life Lenny McLean also fits this triadic underpinning of violence in a very similar way. Although he grew up in a different era and different country, a cultural appreciation of violence, a gendered socialisation around stoic and durable forms of robust masculinity, and incidents of childhood trauma are all present. Each example here – Ray, Bunchy, Lenny – has subtle differences which show how each individual engages in the world. However, enough similarities exist to be able to raise this theory above pathologising the subject and offers something instructive for the criminologist. This is something Josh picks up on in Study-box 7 (see page 89).

Study-box 7

Student Insight:

Meet Josh, a 29-year-old postgraduate student.

The best way to be able to demonstrate one's understanding of complex concepts is to apply them to real world scenarios. Explanations of the relationship between violence and trauma are a great opportunity to begin to try and make these links. Whilst it is important not to use analysis to try and pathologize individuals or be overly deterministic, by using the ultra-realist theory of violence it is possible to analyse the backgrounds of notorious real life or fictional violent offenders. This both demonstrates the utility of the theory as well as furthers one's own understanding. Remember, however, that these explanations do not excuse violent behaviour. Instead, they seek to understand the psyche of violent offenders and how this has developed. When attempting to explain crime and criminality, ultra-realism reminds us that the situation is more complex than solely cultural, psychological or biological factors and a more nuanced approach is needed.

Key Takeaway: Always try and further your understanding by attempting to apply theory and theoretical models to real world scenarios.

Study Questions:

- Can you think of some examples where a propensity for violence can have legitimate instrumental utility?
- Why do Ray and Bunchy respond differently to childhood trauma?
- To what extent can the ultra-realist theory of violence be applied to women?

Key Reading: Ellis, A., Winlow, S. and Hall, S. (2017) ''Throughout My Life I've Had People Walk All Over Me': Trauma in the Lives of Violent Men', *The Sociological Review*, 65 (4), pp. 699-713.

Fig. 7. Study-Box 7.

9

PUTTING ULTRA-REALISM TO WORK

INTRODUCTION

As a theoretical framework, ultra-realism is still quite new and can perhaps be considered a rather modest school of thought (Raymen & Kuldova, 2021). Nevertheless, despite existing on the margins of the mainstream criminological canon, ultra-realism is gaining recognition in some of the discipline's core textbooks (see, for example, Brisman, Carrabine, & South, 2017; Davies, Leighton, & Wyatt, 2021; DeKeseredy & Dragiewicz, 2018; Hopkins Burke, 2018; Liebling, Maruna, & McAra, 2017; Lilly, Cullen, & Ball, 2019; Murphy, 2020). Many of these texts categorise ultra-realism under headings which include terms like 'new directions', 'the birth of new ideas' and 'criminological futures'. Whilst we would argue that ultra-realism certainly occupies a salient position on the frontier of critical criminology, for us its value lies not in its position relevant to the mainstream but rather in its wide-ranging utility. Indeed, perhaps the reason why it is increasingly gaining traction is because more and more scholars recognise the value of drawing upon its insights to explore and explain a range of social scientific phenomena. In this last substantive chapter we aim to highlight some of this innovative scholarship. We begin by looking at work on harmful and violent subjectivities before delving into the expansive realm of deviant leisure. Following this, we consider the concept of harm which is central to ultra-realist work as both an empirical focal point and area of theoretical development. In this vein we also explore how the ultra-realist framework has been applied to analyses of the COVID-19 pandemic. This time, however, rather than drawing upon a film or TV series to help us demonstrate the versatility of ultra-realism, we draw upon the insights offered by the next generation of scholars, our students.

APPLYING ULTRA-REALISM

In Chapter 3 we explored how ultra-realism utilises the philosophy of transcendental materialism to help explain the creation of harmful and criminogenic subjectivities. For those interested in understanding why *some* individuals in *certain* contexts exercise hate and violence, this is both an insightful and important theoretical development. Indeed, James and McBride (2022) have formulated a critical hate studies perspective that is informed by ultra-realism. This new analytical framework endeavours to explain why hate happens in contemporary society and to understand how hate impacts upon the lived experience of victims. Dissatisfied with existing critical theory's inability to explain the breadth of hate behaviours in society (James, 2020), the architects of critical hate studies turned to ultra-realism to facilitate the development of a more nuanced mode of critical thinking on the subject. What makes this perspective particularly useful is that it can be put to work to explain both everyday micro-aggressions directed against multiple and varied groups *and* extreme incidents of hate targeted at those with particular identities. According to James and McBride (2022), extreme incidents of hate are perpetrated by individuals who, in search of an effective Symbolic Order to make sense of their lives, embrace a form of dogma – be it political, religious and/or ideological – that identifies an object upon which to focus their anger. Everyday micro-aggressions, on the other hand, are rooted in the competitive individualism of everyday life. In the absence of an effective Symbolic Order, divisions are created and perceived differences are exacerbated as subjects experience an acute sense of objectless anxiety. People are pitched against each other and hate speech, discrimination and even physical violence may occur as a result (James & McBride, 2022).

Critical hate studies have demonstrated how ultra-realist theorising can be applied to an examination of the nuanced experiences of minority communities, something some ultra-realists have perhaps previously neglected (James, 2020). Indeed, ultra-realism can, and should, be used to challenge a range of biases that exist in contemporary society including, but not limited to, racism, sexism and transphobia. Whilst victims of bias-motivated behaviour are more likely to exist in positions of precarity (James & McBride, 2022), this same position constitutes the backdrop for some violent offenders. Yet, the explanation as to why *some* men are physically violent cannot be solely located in having grown up in marginalised circumstances. There are, as Ellis (2016) points out, broader forces at work here. Adopting a transcendental materialist interpretation of subjectivity and applying insights from the pseudo-pacification process, Ellis (2016) explains that marginalised masculine identities marked by 'toughness' and prone to physical violence are a product of intertwined psychological and socio-economic experiences. For these men, early violent trauma and the residue of shame, coupled with relationships with violent significant others, congeal in the neurological circuitry. As we saw in Chapter 8, these experiences have an impact on the sculpting of their subjectivity and certainly play a part in influencing how they act in the world. Whilst free to make choices and decisions, these are undoubtedly constrained by the socio-economic and cultural conditions within which they reside, where physical violence constitutes an acceptable means of 'getting things done' in a socially atomised and highly competitive society (Ellis, 2016). Indeed, as Ellis (2019, p. 874) notes in later work, lethal and serious violence "appear as unrestrained and often quite extreme manifestations of neoliberal capitalism's disavowed dark heart".

It is becoming increasingly clear that the ultra-realist combination of transcendental materialism and the pseudo-pacification process is a fruitful way of exploring violent and harmful subjectivities in a number of different contexts. Paul, one of our undergraduate students, provides another example:

> *I used ultra-realist theory to analyse the Joker (2019) origin movie. Here the concepts of transcendental materialism and pseudo-pacification were highly effective tools in outlining the process that takes place as Arthur Fleck becomes the Joker, and the impact the political, social and economic context had on this process. I then drew comparisons with the real-world genesis of the mass shooter and how ultra-realism can be used to understand this phenomenon.*

For us, as alluded to in Chapter 3, harmful and/or violent subjectivities are a product of both becoming *and* reversion. Here we of course mean the becoming associated with the transcendental materialist subject, whose synapses are shaped and reshaped in concomitance with their emersion in an environment that cultivates social anxiety, competitive individualism, envy, narcissism and callousness (Wakeman, 2018). We have already seen in Chapter 4 how these functionally aggressive tenets were crucial to the success of the capitalist project and that their cultivation was a core function of the pseudo-pacification process. However, because the pseudo-pacification process now stimulates more aggressive energy than it is capable of pacifying, the regulatory jacket is stretched beyond its limits. In other words, the force of the generative core is eroding the ethico-social constraints that would otherwise regulate and harness this energy to productive purposes. It appears, then, that it is the stimulus associated with *becoming* that contributes to the erosion or *reversion* of the pseudo-pacification's regulatory jacket. We would therefore argue that becoming and reversion exist in a reciprocal relationship apropos the creation of harmful and/or violent subjectivities. Within this context, it is the reproduction of subjectivities attuned to the tenets of the dominant sociosymbolic order that contributes to the erosion of the regulatory jacket. Therefore, as we continue to *become* subjects of a deapted sociosymbolic order so too continues the *reversion* or erosion of ethico-social constraints that help pacify and sublimate subjective forms of harm.

Continuing with the theme of violence, Lynes, Kelly, and Uppal (2019) use ultra-realism to try and revitalise academic work on serial murder. Inspired by the earlier work of Hall and Wilson (2014) on homicide and serial murder, the authors explore the case of Levi Bellfield – the 'bus stop killer'. Through an ultra-realist lens Lynes et al. (2019) account for the macro implications of capitalism on the development of what they call the 'dark flaneur' who operates comfortably in the neo-arcades of non-places and the night-time economy; precisely the environment that facilitated Bellfield's offending. Indeed, "the neo-arcades became the hunting grounds in which the predator first detected the tracks of his prey" (Lynes et al., 2019, p. 533). Crucially, the authors' examination reveals how the modern urban landscape both helps produce serial killers and provides the perfect context for them to operate in.

Ultra-realism has also been applied to the study of the mechanisms through which the general public engage with representations of crime. Yardley, Kelly, and Robinson-Edwards (2019), for example, explore the emergence of the serialised true crime podcast through an ultra-realist lens. The authors plot a course through Lacan's three psychic realms or registers of reality, the Real, the Imaginary and the Symbolic Order, which you may recall from Chapter 3. Initially, true crime depictions of heinous acts facilitate a confrontation with the visceral social realities of the Real. We feel terror, fear and anxiety as we absorb the details of the case (Yardley et al., 2019). At risk of lingering here too long and disengaging, the genre whisks us off into the Imaginary and presents us with a comforting, if not altogether accurate, ending – the villain was apprehended, justice done and we have nothing to fear. The final stage of the journey takes us into the Symbolic Order where collective understandings of the world help assuage our anxiety as we convince ourselves that "we are protected, we are safe, life goes on" (Yardley et al., 2019, p. 508). In this way, the authors question the extent to which these podcasts simply facilitate fetishistic disavowal. We would certainly agree that true crime does not represent a vehicle for change given its location in the Imaginary, where anxieties about the real world are denied (Hall & Winlow, 2015; Yardley et al., 2019).

As part of the ultra-realist arsenal, the Žižekian concept of fetishistic disavowal is an extremely versatile analytical tool which, as we have demonstrated throughout this book, can be applied to a wide range of topics and contexts. Similar to our analysis in Chapter 5, Emma, a postgraduate student, uses this concept in her analysis of *Game of Thrones*:

> *You could argue that the incestuous relationship between Jaime and Cersei Lannister, for the production of 'perfect' heirs, is an example of fetishistic disavowal. This is shown in the casting aside of societal norms to achieve the perception of perfection in terms of the monarchy, influence of familial structure, and overall power.*

Another example comes from Ciaran, a postgraduate student, who utilised the concept in both his undergraduate and postgraduate dissertations:

> *Fetishistic disavowal has appeared in both my undergraduate dissertation surrounding cyberbullying of people over the age of 18, as well as my postgraduate dissertation which explores the harmful impact of gambling mechanics within video games.*

This last example perhaps reflects one of ultra-realism's most enduring legacies, its influence in the development of the deviant leisure perspective. As Winlow (2019) points out, those at the forefront of this perspective have expressed that its roots can be found in ultra-realism. Broadly speaking, the deviant leisure perspective draws attention to the ways in which various forms of harm are structurally embedded within a multitude of accepted and normalised forms of commodified leisure, and how these harms have become culturally accepted (Smith & Raymen, 2018). By drawing on key ultra-realist concepts like special liberty and objectless anxiety, the deviant leisure perspective helps us to explore the motivations of individuals who cause various harms through their commitment to commodified leisure identities (Raymen & Smith, 2019). Despite its relative youth, this insightful framework has been applied to an impressive range of phenomena, including parkour (Raymen, 2019b), urban exploration (Kindynis, 2017), substance use (Ayres, 2019), mass tourism (Large, 2019) and many more (Raymen & Smith, 2019). In Chapter 7 we applied the deviant leisure perspective to our analysis of *Fight Club;* however, for the purposes of this chapter, let us briefly draw attention to two further examples, lifestyle gambling (Raymen & Smith, 2020), and lifestyle drugs (Hall, 2019).

Informed by ongoing ethnographic research among lifestyle gamblers, Raymen and Smith (2019) problematise the positive depiction of 'social' or 'lifestyle' gambling presented in advertising campaigns like the 'Ladbrokes

Life'. In doing so, they shed light on the destructive potential gambling can have on relationships, personal well-being and, of course, one's bank balance. Situated within the context of a consumer culture that encourages us to 'live for the moment' and enjoy *now*, the authors make some interesting points that at first glance appear to run counter to more conventional interpretations of gambling. For example, they point out that rather than being driven by a desire to make profit, "spending money rather than making money was an accepted feature of lifestyle gamblers' narratives" (Raymen & Smith, 2019, p. 388). Indeed, winning bets simply meant the ability to place more bets and spend money on commodities. Moreover, and contrary to what we might think, there also seems to be a palpable dissatisfaction associated with the gambling win. The authors explain this by noting that bets are placed in the *promise* of excitement so that when the win actually comes the excitement surrounding the anticipation of wining vanishes. So, the win, while nice, actually signals the disappearance of the promise (Raymen & Smith, 2019).

In her analysis of the market in lifestyle drugs, or what is also referred to as image and performance enhancing drugs, Hall (2019) also draws on the 'promise' to make sense of why some people consume lifestyle drugs despite the associated risks. Feelings of incompleteness create a desire for things that can potentially fill the void at the heart of the subject. A sense of investment is therefore placed on the promise of the commodity to make us feel complete. In the case of lifestyle drugs, this promise manifests itself through the temporary augmentation of the body and therefore stimulates changes intended to satiate the continuous search for satisfaction. However, as Hall (2019, p. 170) notes, lifestyle drugs "can never fully satisfy the underlying sense of lack". This is because what we find deeply satisfying is actually our dissatisfaction and the enjoyment of trying to escape it, preserving the *promise* of satisfaction. As part of this process, individuals continuously search for more effective products that promise faster and longer-lasting effects (Hall, 2019). By drawing on tools and concepts from cognate fields of study and incorporating these within a broader ultra-realist framework, Hall (2019) contributes to explaining why individuals from multiple walks of life are willing to inflict harm on themselves by using image and performance enhancing drugs.

From these examples we can see how deviant leisure scholars situate the harms they explore within the broader socio-economic and political structures that help produce them. However, rather than forwarding a simple reductionist argument, it is acknowledged that "these political economic structures do not function, and their subsequent harms do not occur, independently of human intervention" (Raymen & Smith, 2020, p. 121). In other words, these harms occur because individual actors, at all levels of society, have developed a subjective willingness to perpetuate existing structures and inflict harm on themselves and/or others – sometimes intentionally and sometimes unintentionally. Ultra-realism is therefore what you might call an indirect expression framework, in that crime and harm are situated within causative *processes* rather than some singular causal mechanism, like an unmediated expression of capitalism, for example (Raymen & Kuldova, 2021). Rather than constituting a closed theory of crime and harm, ultra-realism is "a live and adaptive theoretical *framework*" (Raymen & Kuldova, 2021, p. 246, original emphasis) that can be quite liberating to work with, as Stephen, one of our undergraduates, explains:

> *Ultra-realism is not overly prescriptive. There are no universal laws but 'probabilistic tendencies' which develop under certain conditions (Hall & Winlow, 2015, p. 96). Because of this causal indeterminacy, I felt liberated to approach my work with a sense of freedom, moulding the theoretical components to accentuate the points which best fit my broader arguments. The number of individual parts, which at first felt overwhelming, permitted a nuanced explanation of subtle details. For example, the harms of consumerism range from slight to quite severe. Likewise, our impulse to engage with them varies considerably. For some, lack is a powerful motivator towards crime, for others, it seems to reinforce their commitment to the orthodoxy of paid employment. Where other criminological theories might be too rigid to resolve multiple disparate positions, the flexibility of ultra-realism makes it a very useful framework.*

By now it is perhaps clear that ultra-realism can be put to work to explore both legal and illegal forms of harm. Indeed, Hall and Winlow (2015) emphasise that whilst we should look to move beyond current definitions of 'crime', we should not assume that all current definitions of crime have no relation to real harm.

Ultra-realism demonstrates that the normal, smooth functioning of neoliberal consumer capitalism creates a range of legal harms that have the *probabilistic* power to stimulate illegal responses in ameliorative and/or hyper-conformist capacities (Kotzé, 2019). There can be little doubt that crime and harm exist in a complex relationship as they interact causally and/or effectually with each other. Accordingly, as Kotzé (2018) notes, rather than arbitrarily separating out 'crime' and 'harm' as distinct objects of analytical focus, it perhaps makes more sense to form a more integrated approach towards the study of crime and harm. For Kotzé (2021), ultra-realism is well suited to this task because the core ingredients that comprise it actually demand that we make connections between legal and illegal harm in addressing criminology's *fundamental* question: "why do some individuals and groups risk harm to others as they pursue their instrumental and expressive interests rather than seeking solidarity with one another?" (Hall & Winlow, 2018a, p. 43). Towards this end, Kotzé (2021) positions ultra-realism as a mediating third capable of reviving the dialectic between criminology and zemiology, and, in doing so, providing a firm footing for researching crime and harm.

Focussing on the impact of industrial decline in Teesside, Telford and Lloyd (2020) also identify how entirely legal processes can have harmful and even criminogenic consequences. Deindustrialisation, for example, not only causes harm to individuals and communities but also creates conditions favourable for crime. By drawing attention to the probabilistic causal tendency of absence, the authors trace a variety of legal and illegal harms to what ultra-realists call the negative motivation to harm. That is to say, the largely unintentional harm to communities and individuals generated by the normal functioning of capitalism (Telford & Lloyd, 2020). In his analysis of the service economy of Teesside, Lloyd (2018b) further demonstrates the causative power of absence to generate harm in relation to a reconfigured labour market that puts profit before people. In addition to the absence of stability and security in the workplace, Lloyd (2018b) identifies an absence of moral or ethical responsibility for the Other. This last absence, arguably a product of the previous two, manifests as the positive motivation to harm, where individuals, imbued with a sense of special liberty, would engage in stealing sales and other forms of workplace bullying. Embodying the classic image of the bailiff, these individuals take away from others in order to advance their own position in a highly competitive yet fragile 'winner-take-all' environment (Lloyd, 2018b).

Combining teleological ethics with ultra-realist theory, Raymen (2019a) moves our understanding of social harm forward by outlining a theory of the 'Good'. Essentially, Raymen (2019a) argues that definitional consensus on what actually constitutes social harm is barred by liberal-postmodernism's culture of emotivism. Within this context, belief in any adjudicating authority is suspended in favour of evaluative judgements that simply reflect individual interests and preferences. We can see this play out in our everyday lives. On the one hand, the pollution caused by air traffic and tourism is bad, but on the other, a holiday abroad is *good for me* because I need to de-stress from work. Here, "moral disagreement descends into a manipulative clash of wills" (Raymen, 2019a, p. 140). Therefore, without a shared conception of the

Good, we can have no meaningful consensus on what is, or is not, socially harmful. What we need to work towards, then, is a strong Symbolic Order of shared meanings from which we can pursue the shared goods that are internal to social practices.

The COVID-19 pandemic arguably presented us with an opportunity to usher in a new Symbolic Order capable of sustaining an alternative future, characterised by a greener planet and a fairer and more solidaristic society. However, instead of a coherent and collective vision of an alternative future, Briggs, Ellis, Lloyd, and Telford (2020, p. 844) found only "old futures in disguise" amongst their participants. Drawing on key features of ultra-realism, the authors found that whilst many expressed a sense of optimism and aspiration for a reconfigured future, the ability to act on such sentiment was undermined by the strength of subjective desire for existing consumer lifestyles. With increased online shopping, gaming, Netflix watching and social media surfing, the government's response to the pandemic (lockdown) actually reinforced a commitment to the existing Symbolic Order of consumer capitalism (Briggs et al., 2020).

Evidence suggests that the consequences of lockdowns have been severe as demonstrated by the proliferation of various forms of harm throughout the course of the pandemic; rising levels of domestic abuse, child abuse, hate crime, unemployment and increased mental ill-health (Briggs, Telford, Lloyd, Ellis, & Kotzé, 2021). Whilst not dismissing the risk presented by the virus itself, Briggs et al. (2021) employ an ultra-realist harm framework to highlight, and try to make sense of, the various harms of lockdown. By adopting a more integrated approach that explores both systemic and singular harms, the authors are able to account for the negative *and* positive motivation to harm; demonstrating how they feed into each other to produce both legal and illegal harms. For example, the imposition of restrictions lead to the absence of vital services that exacerbated – and even created new – forms of inequality, as many of the most disadvantaged populations were cut adrift and left to fend for themselves. These unintended harms, reflecting the negative motivation to harm, were accompanied by some demonstrating a willingness to inflict harm on others to satisfy their own expressive and/or instrumental interests. This positive motivation to harm manifested in various ways, from putting others at risk by bulk-buying vital supplies, or not complying with COVID-19 rules, to perpetrating hate crime and sexual and domestic abuse (Briggs et al., 2021).

The utility of ultra-realism as a theoretical and analytical framework is evidently wide-ranging. Throughout this chapter we have demonstrated some of the ways in which it has been put to work to explore and explain some of the most pressing issues of our time. The number of complex moving parts that comprise this interesting perspective give it an impressive analytical range, but it is also what makes it a particularly difficult perspective to get to grips with. The next section demonstrates how some of our students have made sense of ultra-realism and offers some of their insights on effective ways of approaching the subject.

MAKING SENSE OF ULTRA-REALISM

Coupled with an appreciation of how ultra-realism can broaden our perspective of the world in general, and our view of crime and harm in particular, student insights often revealed that a good way to make sense of complex ideas is to try and relate them to your everyday life. Sam, one of our undergraduate students, makes this point really well:

> *When you study criminology at university, you come to realise that many of the bread-and-butter theories were conceived in a very different social world to technologically advanced 21st century consumer society. Ultra-realism takes a good hard look at the face of consumer culture, without blurring out the flaws. Something I have learned from ultra-realism is to broaden my perspective on the traditional ideas of crime and deviance, and to really look at the bigger picture to see the many harms embedded within consumer capitalism. It can initially be difficult to grasp some of ultra-realism's concepts. I found the best way to make sense of it is to apply its teachings to your own understanding of the world. When I have been able to relate my theoretical understanding to my real-world experiences, the penny has dropped.*

This is equally true for those who may encounter ultra-realism for the first time during postgraduate study, as Mark explains:

> *The best theories make clear what is already in view. The pseudo-pacification process and special liberty are two examples of this, because, when reflected upon, the evidence of their relevance can be seen in the experience of your everyday life. You only have to consider your own interactions and observations to find evidence of their existence.*

Evidently, bringing theory into the realm of everyday life not only makes complex ideas easier to grasp but also facilitates a better understanding of how to *apply* theory, thus giving students a greater appreciation of its value (Rothe & Collins, 2013). Emma, one of our postgraduate students who we introduced earlier in this chapter, also echoes this view, noting that "practical examples can help contextualise complex theory".

Something as simple as drawing diagrams can also be a useful way of making sense of theoretical ideas, principles and concepts. Even if you're not what the pedagogical literature calls a 'visual learner', sometimes literally sketching something out on paper is an effective way to grasp what are known as 'threshold concepts'. Serving as conceptual gateways, these concepts open up new and previously inaccessible ways of looking at or thinking about something (Biggs & Tang, 2011). Essentially, once these concepts are understood, a greater level of understanding is attained as the learner "enters new conceptual terrain in which things formally not perceived come into view" (Land, Rattray, & Vivian, 2014, p. 200). This was certainly true for Lauren, our undergraduate from Study-box 6 (see page 77):

> *I found it helpful when taking notes to draw diagrams to help explain some areas, such as transcendental materialism's move from the Real to the Symbolic Order, or the structure of the pseudo-pacification process. It is all about finding out which methods work best for you and sticking to them. Once you get the ball rolling, you can pick it up and understand it quite quickly despite how overwhelming or difficult it may seem at first.*

Reading and engaging with the literature was also identified by our students as being particularly important. When asked to provide one 'key take home message' Mark, for instance, said "read the material, read it again and find something else to read, you will be rewarded". Paul also found that "reading and re-reading various chapters and articles alongside interaction with my tutor in both lectures and seminars really helped it to sink in". When reading, however, Anita, another one of our undergraduates, urges us "not to be intimidated by the tricky concepts of ultra-realism, with patience and perseverance you will understand them". Although the terminology can be a little difficult at times, Anita combined reading with effective note-taking to overcome this obstacle:

> *My strategy for learning the terminology was to pay attention to all lectures and write down any remarks made by the lecturer about the keywords. I also read books and journals recommended by the*

lecturer for the seminar, thereby accumulating additional and useful information for the essays.

There are clearly numerous ways of making sense of complex theories like ultra-realism. However, throughout these informative insights we can detect three main themes which can perhaps be distilled into this key piece of student driven advice: engage with the literature and read as much as you can around the subject; take notes and make diagrams, doodles and other annotations; try and apply aspects of the theory to your everyday life experiences and observations, and, of course, to television shows, films, books and other forms of media.

CONCLUSION

Despite being relatively young, ultra-realism has certainly covered a lot of ground so far. Throughout this chapter we have tried to demonstrate the wide-ranging utility of ultra-realism as a theoretical and analytical framework by highlighting various works that have drawn upon its insights. Indeed, we have seen how ultra-realism has underpinned the development of critical hate studies and the deviant leisure perspective; how it has been used to explore and explain the creation of violent and/or harmful subjectivities; and how it has informed studies on serial murder, true crime, social harm and the COVID-19 pandemic. This is, of course, by no means an exhaustive list of ultra-realist scholarship, but these examples demonstrate how flexible, adaptable and versatile this new theoretical framework is.

The explorative and explanatory power of ultra-realism makes it one of the most exciting perspectives to have emerged in the twenty-first century. However, do not make the mistake of thinking that it is a reductionist or deterministic direct causation theory. Instead, think of it as a perspective that "simply hopes to investigate and shed light upon those contexts that make crime, violence and harm more likely" (Raymen & Kuldova, 2021, p. 246). Towards this end, ultra-realism encourages us to move beyond dated theories that struggle to make sense of the various manifestations of crime and harm in contemporary society. This is not a disparaging comment tinged with a lack of appreciation for our academic forebears. Quite the opposite, it is an acknowledgement that we must demonstrate the same intellectual curiosity that they exhibited and engage in innovative, ambitious and creative social research. The world is changing, and the tools we use to explore and make sense of it need to change too. In time, ultra-realism will also need to continue to evolve or step aside as better theoretical frameworks become available (Winlow, 2019).

For now, however, ultra-realism is helping to, as Paul puts it in Study-box 8 (see page 104), "fill in the gaps that a lot of earlier theory failed to". Moreover, when exposed to new topics, contexts and problems, ultra-realism can be adapted and improved (Raymen & Kuldova, 2021), as we have hopefully demonstrated throughout this chapter. The next generation of scholars will be crucial in the continued development of ultra-realism, and the future certainly looks bright in this regard. We have taught various aspects of this new theory at university for a number of years now, and we continue to be amazed and encouraged by students' engagement with its ideas and the application of them – some of which we have highlighted here and in the various Study-boxes. Yet, like any new subject, engaging with it can be a little scary at times, but it is worth persevering with. If you are coming to the subject for the first time, try using some of the insights offered by our students to help enhance your understanding; and, of course, don't forget to read. To put a L'Oréal Paris twist on Paul's *Key Takeaway* in Study-box 8 (see page 104): Read! Because it's worth it.

Study-box 8

Student Insight:

Meet Paul, a 34-year-old undergraduate student.

I would say that my introduction to ultra-realism was a pretty eye-opening experience. It helped fill in the gaps that a lot of earlier theory failed to. I began using it as a framework to try and understand a variety of criminological and sociological phenomena. For example, I applied key elements to an analysis of the Grenfell Tower fire which I wrote for my Dissertation. The idea that absence can have an equally causative effect as something that is present proved useful when looking at how austerity and deregulation under neoliberalism created the conditions in which such a tragedy could occur. Ideas around positive and negative motivations to harm were also used in my analysis to outline the effect that certain decisions and individual motivations had on the fire taking place.

Key Takeaway: Read, read, read and then read again! For me that was definitely the key to gaining a better understanding of some pretty complex theory. It will take time, but its seriously worth it!

Study Questions:

- Pick either a film or a contemporary social issue and try to apply aspects of ultra-realism to an analysis of it.
- In what ways can ultra-realism be thought of as an indirect expression framework?
- Why should we try to account for both the negative and positive motivation to harm?

Key Reading: James, Z. and McBride, K. (2022) 'Critical Hate Studies: A New Perspective', *International Review of Victimology*, 28 (1), pp. 92-108.

Fig. 8. Study-Box 8.

10

CONCLUSION

We have endeavoured throughout this book to help the reader make sense of ultra-realism. Through the lens of popular culture, from TV series to books and films, we have explored many of the key ingredients, concepts and ideas of this new theoretical framework. It is undoubtedly complex, as is much of the literature that surrounds it, and this is precisely why we have written this book. We hope to have facilitated the flicking of the switch for that lightbulb moment when the seemingly opaque becomes clear. Student testimony tells us that once the light is on it is difficult to turn off, and you may find yourself applying elements of ultra-realism to various social phenomena. Once you grasp the fundamental concepts you will be surprised just how quickly the rest of the puzzle pieces fall into place. Oh, and by the way, you probably will never watch TV and movies in the same way again; to be honest we're not sure if we should apologise for this.

For us, ultra-realism is initially difficult to grasp because it draws upon a range of complex and sometimes mind-boggling ideas and concepts from different disciplines and perspectives. However, it is worth remembering that this is precisely what makes it so versatile, adaptable and penetrative as an analytical tool. As we saw in Chapter 2, ultra-realism has drawn inspiration from the legacies of left realism, critical realism and feminism but moves beyond these frameworks in important ways (Hall & Winlow, 2018a). We are sometimes baffled by the indignation others express at the idea of moving away from theoretical frameworks developed in the twentieth century. To expect that these cutting-edge theories of that time can, and should, effectively explore and explain crime and harm in the twenty-first century is perhaps a little naïve. Besides, is it not also a bit lazy that we resign the aetiological project to history as a job well done by our academic forebears? Surely, a better way to honour their legacy is to continue to question and theorise, using everything at our disposal to try and make sense of the world we live in.

This is the task ultra-realism has set for itself, to explore the experiential realities of everyday life; to dig beneath the surface of abstracted empiricism and relativist emotivism to try and explain the world *as it is* (Kotzé, 2021; Winlow & Hall, 2013). Towards this end great emphasis is placed upon understanding the relationship between the individual subject and the wider sociosymbolic structure, or order. Indeed, as we saw in Chapter 3, the relationship between subject and environment is important because it influences the subjectivisation process. As we act in the world and engage with our external environment, we receive experiential feedback which plays a part in shaping our material composition (Lloyd, 2018b). In other words, we are literally shaped by the material reality of the world we live in. Remember, this is not a one-way street that strips us of our agency. We can also act in the world to shape, influence and change it and as we do those changes provide additional feedback that contributes to shaping our subjectivity. Whilst we are free to act in the world and make choices, ultra-realism acknowledges that our choices are to a large extent constrained by the dominant Symbolic Order. The Symbolic Order and its attendant norms, values and dispositions do not directly determine one's subjectivity, but they *do* make it more *likely* that subjects will embody corresponding characteristics.

This is an important consideration. If, as we have argued here, today's dominant Symbolic Order is characterised by competitive individualism, self-interest, greed and liberal conceptions of freedom, then its subjects are likely to act in ways that reflect these characteristics, with potentially harmful consequences. This interpretation of the ontology of the subject, coupled with insights derived from the cultural-historical theory of the pseudo-pacification process outlined in Chapter 4, allows us to explore both negative and positive motivations to harm in both legal and illegal contexts. In Chapter 9 we demonstrated that for ultra-realism, the smooth functioning of neoliberal consumer capitalism creates a range of legal harms that have the *probabilistic* power to stimulate illegal responses in ameliorative and/or hyper-conformist capacities. This is certainly evident in many of the examples we looked at, including industrial decline, hate crime and various aspects of deviant leisure. What this hopefully demonstrates is that the analytical range of ultra-realism is vast, and, for us, this is one of its core strengths. Indeed, it can be put to work to explore a whole range of issues, identify probabilistic causal chains and highlight connections between phenomena at the macro, meso and micro level.

Dupuy (2013, p. 27) argues that "scientists cannot avoid being the bearers of bad news", perhaps because they have special obligations to 'tell it as it is'.

For its tendency to do so, ultra-realism has sometimes been charged with being overly pessimistic, cynical and bleak in its outlook on life. However, as we noted in Chapter 6, to see such characteristics as inherent to the theory itself is like blaming the mirror for how we look in the morning. Or, stated differently, if you are getting ready for a night out and look in the mirror to make sure your hair looks good, do you fix any strays or simply say, 'this mirror does not accurately reflect me, it's too pessimistic and bleak so I'll buy a new one tomorrow'? The same logic applies here, we should not dismiss the theory because we do not like what it shows us. Throughout the book we have explored a range of issues that may hit close to home: the use of special liberty to satisfy one's self-interest, the structure of lack, desire and consumerist ideology, the fetishistic disavowal of the harms of neoliberal consumer culture and the crises of climate change, violence, hate and even our failure to build something better for everyone out of the ashes of the COVID-19 pandemic. Perhaps ultra-realism is depressing because we see our complicity in some of these issues.

We need to tackle these issues head on, and part of the ultra-realist commitment is to try and determine the level of intervention required to do so. This is not to suggest that ultra-realism is an all-seeing God's eye view of the world (Hall & Winlow, 2015). Proponents of this new theory simply try and cut through existing prohibitions placed on research and theorisation to open up parallax views that might shed some new light on both the symptoms *and* the underlying causes of various issues (Hall & Winlow, 2015). The more traction ultra-realism gains, the broader its analytical reach becomes. This is important because, as Raymen and Kuldova (2021) point out, the more ultra-realism is exposed to new topics, contexts and problems, the more it can be adapted and improved. Established academics, early career researchers and students of all levels are crucial to this constant development. We have tried to demonstrate some of this development here. It is encouraging to see ultra-realism being applied to help explore and explain some very pressing issues by a diverse range of academics. More encouraging, however, is the evidence that this scholarship is beginning to inspire the next generation of academics.

Over the years we have seen both undergraduate and postgraduate students grapple with ultra-realism. This sometimes begins with a little dose of confusion that often accompanies being confronted with complex themes and new ideas. Then, the lightbulb begins to flicker as efforts are made to make sense of this new field of vision and analytical space they have entered. Finally, the flashing is replaced by a steady beam of light reflecting the confident application of the ultra-realist framework to areas of social science of interest to them. We have seen students dig deeper into social injustices like the Grenfell Tower fire, examine the allure and trappings of consumer culture, the harms of gambling, cyberbullying and domestic abuse, and unpick the cultural texts of films like *The Purge*, *Joker* and *The Wolf of Wall Street*. For some, like Maria who we met in Study-box 1, ultra-realism has proved a useful vista from which to make sense of lived experiences in a world influenced by various probabilistic causal tendencies. In pedagogical terms, these students have made discoveries for themselves, adapting what they have learned and applying it to areas of social scientific enquiry. If at least part of our scholarly goal is to promote learning, then this is precisely what we should encourage students to do (Raw, 2016).

From the outset, the aim of this book has been to help make sense of ultra-realism. Towards this end we have emphasised some key elements and core aspects integral to the theory. Sure, the value of this book lies in our efforts to make these more accessible – hopefully. Yet, what adds immeasurable value to this endeavour is the shared experiences of those who have grappled with ultra-realism as students. Their valuable insights, offered in Chapter 9 and the various Study-boxes, provide those coming to the subject for the first time with helpful study suggestions and strategies. These are tried and tested, and, whatever your learning style, you are sure to find some of these insights useful. Reading, sketching out concepts and ideas, creating a reading schedule and working glossary, quizzing yourself and applying the theory to real-world examples are all great ways of helping you engage with, and make sense of, ultra-realism. Remember, it is all about finding what works for you. However, like most things worth pursuing, the one inescapable requirement for making sense of ultra-realism is perseverance. The perseverance to keep reading, keep thinking, keep asking questions and keep exploring. If there was one underlying theme present in the insights offered by our students, this was it.

We hope that this book makes persevering a little easier. Indeed, reading that special liberty is a fantasised state of exception whereby one believes the rules do not apply to them may be a little difficult to grasp at first. However, when paired with a scene from a TV series or movie the concept perhaps becomes a little clearer and easier to understand. For example, consider the subject of special liberty whilst watching Indiana Jones smash the floor of the Church of San Barnaba with a stanchion post to reveal the tomb of Sir Richard in *Indiana Jones and the Last Crusade*. Suddenly our reading that those imbued with a sense of special liberty feel entitled to do whatever it takes to get things done, regardless of the consequences, is played out before us on screen. The concept is made real, more lifelike – even if it is only through the medium of a fictitious character or story – and more relatable, thus rendering it more comprehensible.

This may be the first book-length exploration of ultra-realism through the lens of popular culture, but it is certainly not the first to use popular culture as a vehicle for aiding the comprehension of complex ideas. Indeed, the idea that film, TV shows and other forms of media can provide a comfortable avenue through which to convey complex and sometimes quite abstract concepts has been recognised for some time now (Rothe & Collins, 2013). We would argue that this is not just the case for students but also for established academics who may be coming to the subject for the first time. Accordingly, these colleagues may also find value in the contents of this book. Indeed, whilst we would certainly urge anyone interested in ultra-realism to engage with the seminal texts, this book is perhaps a good place to start. There is, however, also some food for thought for the more experienced reader. For instance, those who are familiar with ultra-realism may want to consider the potential deviation from the theory of violence outlined in Chapter 8, or the idea that harmful and/or violent subjectivities may be a product of both becoming *and* reversion as suggested in Chapter 9.

Like any theory, ultra-realism has its critics (see, for example, Wood, Anderson, & Richards, 2020). Whilst some may offer fair and balanced perspectives, others misinterpret or misrepresent ultra-realism to such an extent that it becomes scarcely recognisable (Raymen & Kuldova, 2021). Dialectical debate is good for the continued development of criminology, but only if it accurately reflects the topic or subject being debated. So, engage with the critique *and* the subject being critiqued and make your own mind up. Having read this attempt at making sense of ultra-realism, move onto the original texts and explore the scholarly works inspired by them, consider the arguments they contain and decide for yourself if the critique is valid or not. One of the key things to remember, however, is that crime and harm do not exist in a vacuum; they cannot be divorced from the wider socio-economic and politico-cultural contexts within which they occur. We need to understand the structure and nature of these contexts and the influence they have on the human subject and our environment. This is not to suggest that these contexts directly or deterministically cause crime and harm in some mechanical fashion. Rather it is to acknowledge that "under certain conditions there are *probabilistic tendencies*" (Hall & Winlow, 2015, p. 96, original emphasis). Accordingly, ultra-realism does not attempt to offer a theory of direct causation, instead it tries to shed light on those things that make crime and harm *more likely* to occur (Raymen & Kuldova, 2021).

What we hope to have made clear here is that the context within which crime and harm occurs is important. It is also highly changeable, and because of this any theory that tries to make sense of social phenomena within this variable context needs to be open and adaptive. So far, ultra-realism has proven itself to be particularly well suited to this task. Indeed, a growing number of academics have demonstrated its utility in facilitating investigations into a broad range of issues; investigations made possible precisely because it is an open theoretical framework rather than a "dogmatic closed cannon of ideas" (Raymen & Kuldova, 2021, p. 260). Its willingness to engage with and mobilise ideas and concepts from other disciplines extends its analytical range and strengthens its explanatory power. Concepts like fetishistic disavowal and enlightened catastrophism are now firmly embedded within the ultra-realist framework. However, ultra-realists do not just incorporate carbon copies of ideas, but they *work with them*, honing and adapting them as they are put to work to help explore contemporary social issues.

Complex though it may be, ultra-realism holds exciting potential not just for criminology but for other social sciences too. As it continues to gain traction and develop as a theoretical framework, it is likely that ultra-realism will facilitate new avenues of investigation that help to elucidate the realities of our time. This is, of course, contingent upon the continued engagement with, and development of, this new framework by academics and students alike. Towards this end, we hope this book offers the intellectually curious with a theoretically rich yet accessible means of making sense of ultra-realism.

REFERENCES

Ayres, T. (2019). Substance use in the night-time economy: Deviant leisure? In T. Raymen & O. Smith (Eds.), *Deviant leisure: Criminological perspectives on leisure and harm* (pp. 135–160). Cham: Palgrave Macmillan.

Badiou, A. (2005). *The century*. Cambridge: Polity Press.

Badiou, A. (2012). *In praise of love*. London: Serpent's Tail.

Bauman, Z. (2007). *Consuming life*. Cambridge: Polity Press.

BBC. (2021). Surge in iPhone sales sees Apple's profits double. *BBC News*, 28 April 2021. Retrieved from https://www.bbc.co.uk/news/business-56920146

Becker, H. (1997). *Outsiders*. New York, NY: Free Press.

Bhaskar, R. (2008). *A realist theory of science*. London: Routledge.

Biggs, J., & Tang, C. (2011). *Teaching for quality learning at university: What the student does* (4th ed.). Maidenhead: Open University Press.

Bognar, G. (2019). Overpopulation and procreative liberty. *Ethics, Policy and Environment*, *22*(3), 319–330.

Bollas, C. (1995). *Cracking up: The work of unconscious experience*. London: Routledge.

Briggs, D. (2020). *Climate changed: Refugee border stories and the business of misery*. London: Routledge.

Briggs, D., Ellis, A., Lloyd, A., & Telford, L. (2020). New hope or old futures in disguise? Neoliberalism, the Covid-19 pandemic and the possibility for social change. *International Journal of Sociology & Social Policy*, *40*(9/10), 831–848.

Briggs, D., & Gamero, R. M. (2017). *Dead end lives*. Bristol: Policy Press.

Briggs, D., Telford, L., Lloyd, A., Ellis, A., & Kotzé, J. (2021). *Lockdown: Social harm in the Covid-19 era*. Cham: Palgrave Macmillan.

Brisman, A., Carrabine, E., & South, N. (Eds.). (2017). *The Routledge companion to criminological theory and concepts*. London: Routledge.

Brown, D. (2014). *Inferno*. London: Corgi Books.

Carrabine, E. (2008). *Crime, culture and the media*. Cambridge: Polity Press.

Claisse, F., & Delvenne, P. (2015). Building on anticipation: Dystopia as empowerment. *Current Sociology Monograph*, *63*(2), 155–169.

Collier, A. (1994). *Critical realism: An introduction to Roy Bhaskar's philosophy*. London: Verso.

Currie, E. (1985). *Confronting crime: An American challenge*. New York, NY: Pantheon.

Currie, E. (1997). Market, crime and community: Towards a mid-range theory of post-industrial violence. *Theoretical Criminology*, *1*(2), 147–172.

Davey, J. (2021). Britain on track for record Black Friday sales. *Reuters*, 26 November 2021. Retrieved from https://www.reuters.com/business/retail-consumer/shortages-cast-shadow-over-britains-black-friday-2021-11-26/

Davies, P., Leighton, P., & Wyatt, T. (Eds.). (2021). *The Palgrave handbook of social harm*. Cham: Palgrave Macmillan.

Davis, A. C., Arnocky, S., & Stroink, M. (2019). The problem of overpopulation: Proenvironmental concerns and behaviour predict reproductive attitudes. *Ecopsychology*, *11*(2), 92–100.

DeKeseredy, W. S., & Dragiewicz, M. (Eds.). (2018). *Routledge handbook of critical criminology* (2nd ed.). London: Routledge.

Ditton, J. (1979). *Controlology*. London: Macmillan.

Dupuy, J. P. (2009). The precautionary principle and enlightened doomsaying: Rational choice before the apocalypse. *Occasion: Interdisciplinary Studies in the Humanities*, *1*(1), 1–13.

Dupuy, J. P. (2013). *The mark of the sacred*. Stanford, CA: Stanford University Press.

Dupuy, J. P. (2014). *Economy and the future: A crisis of faith*. East Lansing: Michigan State University Press.

Dupuy, J. P. (2015). *A short treatise on the metaphysics of tsunamis*. East Lansing, MI: Michigan State University Press.

Eagleton, T. (2009). *Trouble with strangers: A study of ethics*. Chichester: Wiley-Blackwell.

Elias, N. (2000). *The civilising process: Sociogenetic and psychogenetic investigations* (Revised edition). Oxford: Blackwell.

Ellis, A. (2016). *Men, masculinities and violence: An ethnographic study*. London: Routledge.

Ellis, A. (2019). A decivilizing reversal or system normal? Rising lethal violence in post-recession austerity United Kingdom. *British Journal of Criminology*, *59*(4), 862–878.

Ellis, A., Briggs, D., Winlow, S., Esquinas, A. S., Verdugo, R. C., & Suárez, J. R. P. (2018). Liberalism, lack and living the dream: Re-considering youth, consumer sovereignty and the attractions of night-time leisure in Magaluf. *Journal of Extreme Anthropology*, *2*(2), 22–41.

Ellis, A., Winlow, S., & Hall, S. (2017). 'Throughout my life I've had people walk all over me': Trauma in the lives of violent men. *The Sociological Review*, *65*(4), 699–713.

Feeley, M. M., & Simon, J. (1992). The new penology: Notes on the emerging strategy of corrections and its implications. *Criminology*, *30*(4), 449–474.

Ferrell, J., Hayward, K., & Young, J. (2015). *Cultural criminology: An invitation* (2nd ed.). London: Sage.

Fisher, M. (2009). *Capitalist realism: Is there no alternative?* Winchester: Zero Books.

Foucault, M. (1977). *Discipline and punish: The birth of the prison*. London: Penguin Books.

Freud, S. (2003). *Beyond the pleasure principle*. London: Penguin Books.

Fuggle, S. (2018). In search of temporal loopholes: Insuring against a future that will never come. *Continuum: Journal of Media & Cultural Studies*, *32*(6), 795–807.

Gadd, S., & Jefferson, T. (2007). *Psychosocial criminology: An introduction*. London: Sage.

Giroux, H. (2001). Private satisfactions and public disorders: *Fight club*, patriarchy, and the politics of masculine violence. *Journal of Antimicrobial Chemotherapy*, *21*(1), 1–31.

Hall, A. (2019). Lifestyle drugs and late capitalism: A topography of harm. In T. Raymen & O. Smith (Eds.), *Deviant leisure: Criminological perspectives on leisure and harm* (pp. 161–186). Cham: Palgrave Macmillan.

Hall, S. (1997). Visceral cultures and criminal practices. *Theoretical Criminology*, *1*(4), 453–478.

Hall, S. (2000). Paths to anelpis, 1: Dimorphic violence and the pseudo-pacification process. *Parallax: A Journal of Metadiscursive Theory and Cultural Practices*, *6*(2), 36–53.

Hall, S. (2002). Daubing the drudges of fury: Men, violence and the piety of the 'hegemonic masculinity' thesis. *Theoretical Criminology*, *6*(1), 35–61.

Hall, S. (2007). The emergence and breakdown of the pseudo-pacification process. In K. D. Watson (Ed.), *Assaulting the past: Violence and civilization in historical context* (pp. 77–101). Newcastle: Cambridge Scholars Publishing.

Hall, S. (2012a). *Theorizing crime and deviance: A new perspective*. London: Sage.

Hall, S. (2012b). Don't look up, don't look down: Liberal criminology's fear of the supreme and the subterranean. *Crime, Media, Culture*, *8*(2), 197–212.

Hall, S. (2012c). Consumer culture and the meaning of the urban riots in England. In S. Hall & S. Winlow (Eds.), *New directions in criminological theory* (pp. 145–164). London: Routledge.

Hall, S. (2012d). The solicitation of the trap: On transcendence and transcendental materialism in advanced consumer-capitalism. *Human Studies*, *35*(3), 365–381.

Hall, S. (2013). Living it down in Havana: Organized crime and the pseudo-pacification process. In S. Winlow & R. Atkinson (Eds.), *New directions in crime and deviancy* (pp. 40–54). London: Routledge.

Hall, S. (2014). Social deviance. In M. Sasaki, J. Goldstone, E. Zimmermann, & S. K. Sanderson (Eds.), *Concise encyclopaedia of comparative sociology* (pp. 402–409). Leiden: Brill.

Hall, S. (2015). What is criminology about? The study of harm, special liberty and pseudo-pacification in late-capitalism's libidinal economy. In D. Crewe & R. Lippens (Eds.), *What is criminology about? Philosophical reflections* (pp. 122–140). London: Routledge.

Hall, S. (2020). Consumer culture and English history's lost object. In S. Hall, T. Kuldova, & M. Horsley (Eds.), *Crime, harm and consumerism* (pp. 21–38). London: Routledge.

Hall, S., Kuldova, T., & Horsley, M. (2020). Introduction. In S. Hall, T. Kuldova, & M. Horsley (Eds.), *Crime, harm and consumerism* (pp. 1–18). London: Routledge.

Hall, S., & Wilson, D. (2014). New foundations: Pseudo-pacification and special liberty as potential cornerstones for a multi-level theory of homicide and serial murder. *European Journal of Criminology, 11*(5), 635–655.

Hall, S., & Winlow, S. (2004). Barbarians at the gate: Crime and violence in the breakdown of the pseudo-pacification process. In J. Ferrell, K. Hayward, W. Morrison, & M. Presdee (Eds.), *Cultural criminology unleashed* (pp. 275–286). London: Glasshouse Press.

Hall, S., & Winlow, S. (2007). Cultural criminology and primitive accumulation: A formal introduction for two strangers who should really become more intimate. *Crime, Media, Culture*, *3*(1), 82–90.

Hall, S., & Winlow, S. (2012). Introduction: The need for new directions in criminological theory. In S. Hall & S. Winlow (Eds.), *New directions in criminological theory* (pp. 1–13). London: Routledge.

Hall, S., & Winlow, S. (2015). *Revitalizing criminological theory: Towards a new ultra-realism.* London: Routledge.

Hall, S., & Winlow, S. (2018a). Ultra-realism. In W. S. DeKeseredy & M. Dragiewicz (Eds.), *Routledge handbook of critical criminology* (2nd ed., pp. 43–56). London: Routledge.

Hall, S., & Winlow, S. (2018b). Big trouble or little evils: The ideological struggle over the concept of harm. In A. Boukli & J. Kotzé (Eds.), *Zemiology: Reconnecting crime and social harm* (pp. 107–126). Cham: Palgrave Macmillan.

Hall, S., Winlow, S., & Ancrum, C. (2008). *Criminal identities and consumer culture: Crime, exclusion and the new culture of narcissism.* Cullompton: Willan Publishing.

Harvey, D. (2010). *The enigma of capital.* London: Profile.

Haywood, R., & Spivak, R. (2012). *Maritime piracy.* London: Routledge.

Heidensohn, F. (2012). The future of feminist criminology. *Crime, Media, Culture*, *8*(2), 123–134.

Hopkins-Burke, R. (2018). *An introduction to criminological theory* (5th ed.). London: Routledge.

Horkheimer, M., & Adorno, T. (1997). *Dialectic of enlightenment*. London: Verso.

Horsley, M. (2015). *The dark side of prosperity*. Farnham: Ashgate.

Horsley, M., Kotzé, J., & Hall, S. (2015). The maintenance of orderly disorder: Modernity, markets and the pseudo-pacification process. *Journal on European History of Law*, *6*(1), 18–29.

Horsley, M., & Lloyd, A. (2020). Mass indebtedness and the luxury of payment means. In S. Hall, T. Kuldova, & M. Horsley (Eds.), *Crime, harm and consumerism* (pp. 73–89). London: Routledge.

James, O. (2008). *The selfish capitalist: Origins of affluenza*. London: Vermilion.

James, Z. (2020). Gypsies' and travellers' lived experience of harm: A critical hate studies perspective. *Theoretical Criminology*, *24*(3), 502–520.

James, Z., & McBride, K. (2022). Critical hate studies: A new perspective. *International Review of Victimology*, *28*(1), 92–108.

Johnston, A. (2008). *Žižek's ontology: A transcendental materialist theory of subjectivity*. Evanston: Northwestern University Press.

Johnston, A., & Malabou, C. (2013). *Self and emotional life: Philosophy, psychoanalysis, and neuroscience*. New York, NY: Columbia University Press.

Kara, S. (2018). Is your phone tainted by the misery of the 35,000 children in Congo's mines? *The Guardian*, 12 October 2018. Retrieved from https://www.theguardian.com/global-development/2018/oct/12/phone-misery-children-congo-cobalt-mines-drc

Kindynis, T. (2017). Urban exploration: From subterranea to spectacle. *British Journal of Criminology*, *57*(4), 982–1001.

Kotzé, J. (2018). Criminology or zemiology? Yes, please! On the refusal of choice between false alternatives. In A. Boukli & J. Kotzé (Eds.), *Zemiology: Reconnecting crime and social harm* (pp. 85–106). Cham: Palgrave Macmillan.

Kotzé, J. (2019). *The myth of the 'crime decline': Exploring change and continuity in crime and harm*. London: Routledge.

Kotzé, J. (2020). The commodification of abstinence. In S. Hall, T. Kuldova, & M. Horsley (Eds.), *Crime, harm and consumerism* (pp. 54–69). London: Routledge.

Kotzé, J. (2021). On researching harm: An ultra-realist perspective. In P. Davies, P. Leighton, & T. Wyatt (Eds.), *The Palgrave handbook of social harm* (pp. 117–138). Cham: Palgrave Macmillan.

Kotzé, J., & Antonopoulos, G. A. (2021). Boosting bodily capital: Maintaining masculinity, aesthetic pleasure and instrumental utility through the consumption of steroids. *Journal of Consumer Culture*, *21*(3), 683–700.

Kotzé, J., Richardson, A., & Antonopoulos, G. A. (2020). Looking 'acceptably' feminine: A single case study of a female bodybuilder's use of steroids. *Performance Enhancement and Health*, *8*(2–3), 100174. doi:10.1016/j.peh.2020.100174

Kuldova, T. (2019). Fetishism and the problem of disavowal. *Qualitative Market Research: An International Journal*, *22*(5), 766–780.

Land, R., Rattray, J., & Vivian, P. (2014). Learning in the liminal space: A semiotic approach to threshold concepts. *Higher Education*, *67*(2), 199–217.

Large, J. (2018). Spot the fashion victim(s): The importance of rethinking harm within the context of fashion counterfeiting. In A. Boukli & J. Kotzé (Eds.), *Zemiology: Reconnecting crime and social harm* (pp. 223–243). Cham: Palgrave Macmillan.

Large, J. (2019). Conspicuously 'doing' charity: Exploring the relationship between doing good and doing harm in tourism. In T. Raymen & O. Smith (Eds.), *Deviant leisure: Criminological perspectives on leisure and harm* (pp. 325–345). Cham: Palgrave Macmillan.

Lea, J., & Young, J. (1993). *What is to be done about law and order?* (2nd ed.). London: Pluto Press.

Liebling, A., Maruna, S., & McAra, L. (Eds.). (2017). *The Oxford handbook of criminology* (6th ed.). Oxford: Oxford University Press.

Lilly, J. R., Cullen, F. T., & Ball, R. A. (2019). *Criminological theory: Context and consequences* (7th ed.). London: Sage.

Lizardo, O. (2007). *Fight club*, or the cultural contradictions of late capitalism. *Journal for Cultural Research*, *11*(3), 221–243.

Lloyd, A. (2012). Working to live, not living to work: Work, leisure and identity among call centre workers in North East England. *Current Sociology*, *60*(5), 619–635.

Lloyd, A. (2017). Ideology at work: Reconsidering ideology, the labour process and workplace resistance. *International Journal of Sociology & Social Policy, 37*(5/6), 266–279.

Lloyd, A. (2018a). Serving up harm: Systemic violence, transitions to adulthood and the service economy. In A. Boukli & J. Kotzé (Eds.), *Zemiology: Reconnecting crime and social harm* (pp. 245–264). Cham: Palgrave Macmillan.

Lloyd, A. (2018b). *The harms of work: An ultra-realist account of the service economy*. Bristol: Bristol University Press.

Lloyd, A. (2020). Harm at work: Bullying and special liberty in the retail sector. *Critical Criminology, 28*(4), 669–683.

Lloyd, A., & Horsley, M. (2021). *Consumer culture, precarious incomes and mass indebtedness: Borrowing from uncertain futures, consuming in precarious times*. Thesis Eleven. doi:10.1177%2F07255136211053421

Lynes, A., Kelly, C., & Uppal, P. K. S. (2019). Benjamin's 'Flâneur' and serial murder: An ultra-realist literary case study of Levi Bellfield. *Crime, Media, Culture, 15*(3), 523–543.

Marx, K. (1990). *Capital* (Vol. 1). Oxford: Oxford University Press.

Marx, K., & Engels, F. (1998). *The German ideology*. New York, NY: Prometheus Books.

McChesney, R. W. (1999). Introduction. In N. Chomsky, *Profit over people: Neoliberalism and global order* (pp. 7–16). New York, NY: Seven Stories Press.

McGowan, T. (2016). *Capitalism and desire: The psychic cost of free markets*. New York, NY: Columbia University Press.

McLean, L. (1998). *The Guv'nor*. London: Blake Publishing.

Merchant, B. (2018). *The one device: The secret history of the iPhone*. London: Corgi Books.

Milbank, J., & Pabst, A. (2018). *The politics of virtue: Post-liberalism and the human future*. London: Rowman & Littlefield.

Miles, S. (1998). *Consumerism as a way of life*. London: Sage.

Murphy, T. (2020). *Criminology: A contemporary introduction*. London: Sage.

Myers, T. (2003). *Slavoj Žižek*. London: Routledge.

Neyrat, F. (2019). Ghosts of extinction: An essay in spectral ecopolitics. *Oxford Literary Review*, *41*(1), 88–106.

Palahniuk, C. (1996/2006). *Fight club*. London: Vintage.

Parenti, C. (2011). *Tropic of chaos: Climate change and the new geography of violence*. New York, NY: Nation Books.

Pemberton, S. (2016). *Harmful societies*. Bristol: Policy Press.

Piketty, T. (2014). *Capital in the twenty-first century*. London: Belknap.

Pinker, S. (2012). *The better angels of our nature*. London: Penguin Books.

Pitron, G. (2020). *The rare metals war*. London: Scribe.

Rafter, N. (2007). Crime, film and criminology: Recent sex-crime movies. *Theoretical Criminology*, *11*(3), 403–420.

Raw, L. (2016). Adaptive pedagogies and paragogies. *Transformations: The Journal of Inclusive Scholarship and Pedagogy*, *26*(1), 89–99.

Raymen, T. (2016). Designing-in crime by designing-out the social? Situational crime prevention and the intensification of harmful subjectivities. *British Journal of Criminology*, *56*(3), 497–514.

Raymen, T. (2018). Living in the end times through popular culture: An ultra-realist analysis of *the walking dead* as popular criminology. *Crime, Media, Culture*, *14*(3), 429–447.

Raymen, T. (2019a). The enigma of social harm and the barrier of liberalism: Why zemiology needs a theory of the good. *Justice, Power and Resistance*, *3*(1), 133–162.

Raymen, T. (2019b). *Parkour, deviance and leisure in the late-capitalist city: An ethnography*. Bingley: Emerald Publishing.

Raymen, T., & Kuldova, T. (2021). Clarifying ultra-realism: A response to Wood et al. *Continental Thought and Theory: A Journal of Intellectual Freedom*, *3*(2), 242–263.

Raymen, T., & Smith, O. (2016). 'What's deviance got to do with it? Black Friday sales, violence and hyper-conformity. *British Journal of Criminology*, *56*(2), 389–405.

Raymen, T., & Smith, O. (2019). Deviant leisure: A critical criminological perspective for the twenty-first century. *Critical Criminology*, *27*(1), 115–130.

Raymen, T., & Smith, O. (2020). Lifestyle gambling, indebtedness and anxiety: A deviant leisure perspective. *Journal of Consumer Culture*, *20*(4), 381–399.

Raymen, T., & Smith, O. (2021). The post-Covid future of the environmental crisis industry and its implications for green criminology and zemiology. *Journal of Contemporary Crime, Harm and Ethics*, *1*(1), 63–87.

Robins, N. (2012). *The corporation that changed the world: How the East India Company shaped the modern multinational* (2nd ed.). London: Pluto Press.

Rothe, D. L., & Collins, V. E. (2013). Teaching criminological theory: The power of film and music. *Critical Criminology*, *21*(2), 227–241.

Smaligo, N. (2014). *The occupy movement explained: From corporate control to democracy*. Chicago, IL: Open Court Publishing.

Smith, O. (2014). *Contemporary adulthood and the night-time economy*. Basingstoke: Palgrave Macmillan.

Smith, O., & Raymen, T. (2017). Shopping with violence: Black Friday sales in the British context. *Journal of Consumer Culture*, *17*(3), 677–694.

Smith, O., & Raymen, T. (2018). Deviant leisure: A criminological perspective. *Theoretical Criminology*, *22*(1), 63–82.

Streeck, W. (2016). *How will capitalism end?* London: Verso.

Ta, L. M. (2006). Hurt so good: *Fight club*, masculine violence, and the crisis of capitalism. *Journal of American Culture*, *29*(3), 265–277.

Tarnas, R. (2010). *The passion of the western mind: Understanding the ideas that have shaped our world view*. London: Pimlico.

Taylor, J. D. (2013). *Negative capitalism: Cynicism in the neoliberal era*. Winchester: Zero Books.

Taylor, I., Walton, P., & Young, J. (2013). *The new criminology: For a social theory of deviance* (40th anniversary edition). London: Routledge.

Telford, L. (2022). *English nationalism and its ghost towns*. London: Routledge.

Telford, L., & Lloyd, A. (2020). From "Infant Hercules" to "Ghost Town": Industrial collapse and social harm in Teesside. *Critical Criminology*, *28*, 595–611.

Treadwell, J., Briggs, D., Winlow, S., & Hall, S. (2013). Shopocalypse now: Consumer culture and the English riots of 2011. *British Journal of Criminology*, *53*(1), 1–17.

Tudor, K. (2018). Toxic sovereignty: Understanding fraud as the expression of special liberty within late-capitalism. *Journal of Extreme Anthropology*, *2*(2), 1–15.

Tudor, K. (2019). Symbolic survival and harm: Serious fraud and consumer capitalism's perversion of the causa sui project. *The British Journal of Criminology*, *59*(5), 1237–1253.

Ugwudike, P. (2015). *An introduction to critical criminology*. Bristol: Policy Press.

Vold, G. B., Bernard, T. J., & Snipes, J. B. (2002). *Theoretical criminology* (5th ed.). Oxford: Oxford University Press.

Wakeman, S. (2018). The one who knocks and the one who waits: Gendered violence in breaking bad. *Crime, Media, Culture*, *14*(2), 213–228.

Wattis, L. (2021). The cultural scope and criminological potential of the 'hardman story'. *Crime, Media, Culture*. doi:10.1177%2F17416590211053795

Whitehead, P. (2015). *Reconceptualising the moral economy of criminal justice: A new perspective*. Basingstoke: Palgrave Macmillan.

Whitehead, P. (2018). *Demonising the other: The criminalisation of morality*. Bristol: Policy Press.

Wieviorka, M. (2009). *Violence: A new approach*. London: Sage.

Wilson, J. Q. (2013). *Thinking about crime* (Revised edition). New York, NY: Basic Books.

Winlow, S. (2001). *Badfellas: Crime, tradition and new masculinities*. Oxford: Berg.

Winlow, S. (2013). Is it OK to talk about capitalism again? Or, why criminology must take a leap of faith. In S. Winlow & R. Atkinson (Eds.), *New directions in crime and deviancy* (pp. 21–39). London: Routledge.

Winlow, S. (2014). Trauma, guilt and the unconscious: Some theoretical notes on violent subjectivity. *The Sociological Review*, *62*(S2), 32–49.

Winlow, S. (2017). The uses of catastrophism. In R. Atkinson, L. McKenzie, & S. Winlow (Eds.), *Building better societies: Promoting social justice in a world falling apart* (pp. 179–192). Bristol: Policy Press.

Winlow, S. (2019). What lies beneath? Some notes on ultra-realism, and the intellectual foundations of the 'deviant leisure' perspective. In T. Raymen & O. Smith (Eds.), *Deviant leisure: Criminological perspectives on leisure and harm* (pp. 45–65). Cham: Palgrave Macmillan.

Winlow, S., & Hall, S. (2006). *Violent night: Urban leisure and contemporary culture*. Oxford: Berg.

Winlow, S., & Hall, S. (2009). Retaliate first: Memory, humiliation and male violence. *Crime, Media, Culture*, *5*(3), 285–304.

Winlow, S., & Hall, S. (2013). *Rethinking social exclusion: The end of the social?* London: Sage.

Winlow, S., & Hall, S. (2016). Realist criminology and its discontents. *International Journal for Crime, Justice and Social Democracy*, *5*(3), 80–94.

Winlow, S., & Hall, S. (2019). Shock and awe: On progressive minimalism and retreatism, and the new ultra-realism. *Critical Criminology*, *27*(1), 21–36.

Winlow, S., Hall, S., Treadwell, J., & Briggs, D. (2015). *Riots and political protest: Notes from the post-political present*. London: Routledge.

Wolin, R. (2010). *The wind from the east*. Oxford: Princeton University Press.

Wood, M., Anderson, B., & Richards, I. (2020). Breaking down the pseudo-pacification process: Eight critiques of ultra-realist crime causation theory. *British Journal of Criminology*, *60*(3), 642–661.

Yardley, E., Kelly, E., & Robinson-Edwards, S. (2019). Forever trapped in the imaginary of late capitalism? The serialized true crime podcast as a wake-up call in times of criminological slumber. *Crime, Media, Culture*, *15*(3), 503–521.

Žižek, S. (1989). *The sublime object of ideology*. London: Verso.

Žižek, S. (2000). Da capo senza fine. In J. Butler, E. Laclau, & S. Žižek (Eds.), *Contingency, hegemony, universality: Contemporary dialogues on the left* (pp. 213–262). London: Verso.

Žižek, S. (2006). *How to read lacan*. London: Granta Books.

Žižek, S. (2008). *The ticklish subject: The absent centre of political ontology*. London: Verso.

Žižek, S. (2009). *Violence: Six sideways reflections*. London: Profile Books.

Žižek, S. (2017). *The courage of hopelessness: Chronicles of a year of acting dangerously*. London: Allen Lane.

Žižek, S. (2020). *Pandemic: Covid-19 shakes the world*. London: OR Books.

INDEX

Printed in the United States
by Baker & Taylor Publisher Services